MAN ALIVE!

Dressing the Free Way

CHARLES HIX

Photography by
Stephen AuCoin

Styling by
Gail Sadow

SIMON AND SCHUSTER
New York

Published by Simon and Schuster
A Division of Simon & Schuster, Inc.
Simon & Schuster Building
Rockefeller Center
1230 Avenue of the Americas
New York, New York 10020
SIMON AND SCHUSTER and colophon are registered trademarks
of Simon & Schuster, Inc.
Designed by Hix/Metz
Production directed by Richard L. Willett
Manufactured in the United States of America

1 2 3 4 5 6 7 8 9 10

Library of Congress Cataloging in Publication Data
ISBN 0-671-50085-6

The following models appear in the Front Matter of *Man Alive!* Page 1, left: Richard Villella; right: Jim Catch. Page 2, John Sommi. Page 3, Brian Terrell. Page 4, upper right: Terrence Dineen; lower right: Todd Bentley. Page 5, John Henry. Page 6, both photos: Benjamin Hobbins. Page 7, both photos: Noa. On Page 230, the models are: Patrick Taylor, upper photo; Pat Hardie, lower photo.

TO

STEVE & GAIL
(because never has there been such a
partnership)

THE MODELS
(because without them this wouldn't be)

THE MODEL AGENCIES & THE
BOOKERS
(because they were generous and able: in New
York—Click, Elite, Ford, Model & Talent Group,
Video Talent, Wilhelmina & Zoli; in Fort
Lauderdale—City Models; in Milan—Model
Plan)

BOB
(because he's the most reassuring—and droll—
of editors)

EVE
(because her door is always open)

LYNN
(because of the faith and the bucks)

PAT
(because she is loving)

MOM & DAD
(because I'm here and they approve)

BOB
(because he's Bob and that makes all the
difference)

CONTENTS

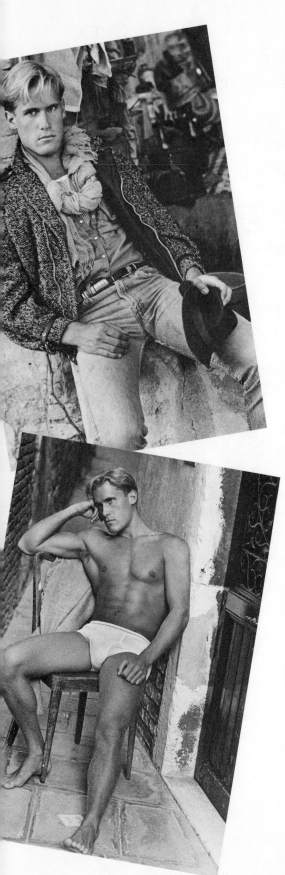

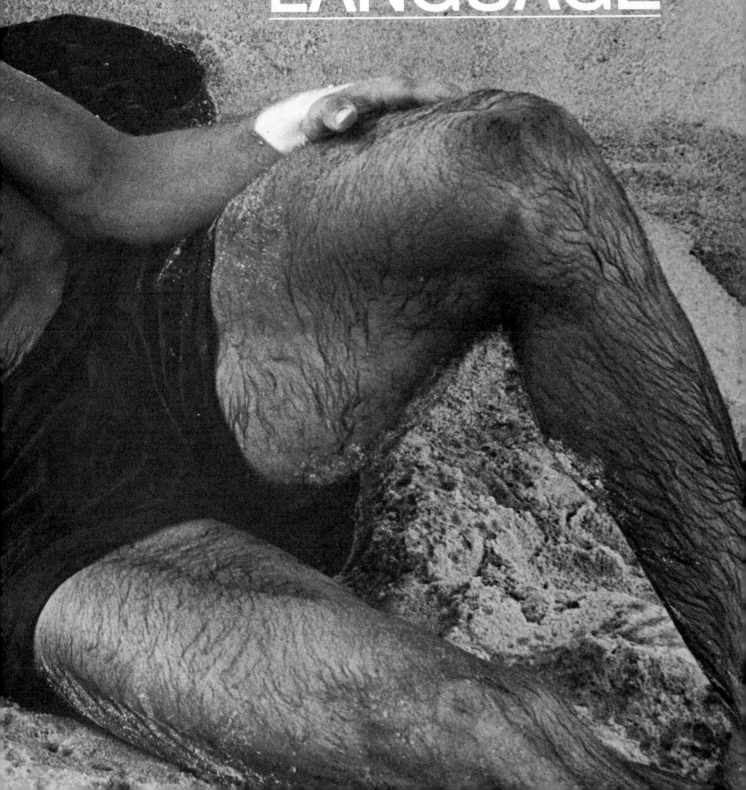

INTRODUCTION
BODY LANGUAGE

BARE TRUTH

You probably don't know why you dress the way you do. In fact, you probably don't know why you wear clothes at all. You may assume you dress to withstand a nasty breeze or simply to stay out of the slammer. Those reasons don't explain why you wear a shirt and trousers instead of a bear skin or a toga.

Clothing was invented for reasons other than merely conserving body heat or concealing genitalia. In cold climates, primitive men and women did wear bear skins to protect their bare skins. But in some tropical zones, native attire consisted of shark's-tooth necklaces and little else. Initially, clothing was steeped in superstition and myth, in magical lore. Blue body paint was the "dress" of ancient Egyptian royalty. Even today, Australian bushmen "clothe" themselves with patterns of colored clay applied directly to their exposed skin.

With the advent of "enlightened civilization," clothing's primary purpose was to distinguish between the sexes, and that is still true: it's comedic or shocking to see a man in an organdy evening gown because men are supposed to wear men's clothing; although given more latitude, women are also expected to stick mainly to women's apparel. When members of either sex don't dress in their sexually assigned garb, the situation becomes topsy-turvy. During less liberated days, a person could be jailed not only for failing to wear clothes appropriate to his or her gender but also for committing the blasphemous crime of donning taboo colors.

An afternoon spent examining portraiture in an art museum can yield the self-evident conclusion that styles in clothing change. Less obviously, the shifting styles of dress depicted in art indicate something about the social atmosphere during which the portraits were painted. During the mid-nineteenth century in Britain, for example, men of the Victorian era posed in somber, slightly oversized clothing

PRECEDING DOUBLE-PAGE SPREAD. Clothing both conceals and reveals various parts of the human body. In off-duty garb society sanctions greater visibility of the male chest and legs than is ever acceptable in on-duty garb unless a man is a lifeguard or a professional athlete. Model: Richard Villella.

LEFT. Many people mistakenly believe clothing was invented for genital coverage. A towel can manage that feat. Why certain types and styles of clothing are worn is explained more by socially imposed and trained role-playing than by mere modesty. Model: Neil Neuhaus.

which proclaimed them to be solid, practical men of substance. A "proper gentleman" of that period dressed in a manner that reflected the work-prized values of Victorian society. That clothing was very different from the masculine garb worn a century earlier. Then, men (as well as women) paraded in elaborate costumes aglitter with gilt and aflutter with lace—attire proclaiming the luxurious wealth and indolent leisure of the aristocracy as distinguished from the functional homespun garb of the rough-hewn masses who tilled the soil and could not afford to have their portraits painted: ostentatious wealth, blue blood and conspicuous leisure were treasured; common labor was disdained.

In centuries past, whatever the prevailing mode of the moment, clothing designers didn't dictate what people of any particular period wore, and they still don't today. If designers really possessed the power to transform fashion at the whimsical snap of their fingers, styles would change much more rapidly and drastically than they do. The fact is, men's clothing styles actually change relatively slowly, since society seldom moves swiftly to redefine itself. Seen in its broadest context, clothing reflects societal conceptions about the roles of men and women in the scheme of things. Clothing symbolizes social values, the etiquette of the times. When someone isn't dressed in a socially acceptable manner, he or she simply isn't socially acceptable. The trick is knowing what is acceptable—and what isn't—under prescribed conditions. Only in a nudist camp is clothing selection totally foolproof.

STREET SMART

Clothing does more than instruct us on the acceptable roles for men and women of any period. How closely individuals approximate or deviate from the conventional style of the period also informs us about those individuals. Take today, for instance. Imagine a man wearing a navy blue pin-striped suit, a white button-down-collared shirt and a blue-and-maroon striped silk tie.

When that imagined man is placed in an office building, we conclude that he is an industrious worker, probably at management level, who desires corporate success.

When the same imagined man is placed inside a seedy strip joint, we conclude he's a traveling salesman out for a cheap thrill and probably a fast pickup.

Now imagine a man in blue jeans and a sweat shirt. Place this imagined man in an office building and we conclude that he works in the mail room. Put him in a seedy strip joint and we think him a regular.

What someone wears conveys a great deal of information about him or her even when he or she is a perfect stranger. However, when dealing with strangers, we don't know whether the information transmitted is true or false, purposeful or accidental.

Let's return to our imaginary fellow in the navy blue pin-striped suit. Give him an attaché case. Should we see him walking on Wall Street, we conclude that he's a professional man, possibly a stockbroker. That may be true. Or perhaps he's a job applicant who read in a magazine that the best way to get a job on Wall Street is to dress for the interview as if he already worked there. Or maybe he's the well-groomed robber who has been stealing successfully from a string of brokerage houses; in his attaché case he is carrying not Dow Jones reports but a gun with a silencer.

We seldom take the time to ponder why someone is dressed in a particular style. We merely assume that that's the way the person wants to be seen . . . and judged. Without articulating our judgments in words or even conscious thought, we make a variety of conclusions about others based solely on their dress. When we see a man strolling along the street in a bright yellow tie, we automatically think him a cheery, optimistic fellow. We assume he has freely chosen to announce his true feelings as represented by his tie. Since we're responding on a subliminal level, we "hear" the tale the yellow tie subconsciously relates to us . . . even though it may be that the fellow's wife insisted that he wear that yellow tie, he in fact has murderous thoughts in his mind. Unless we are introduced to the man and discover his foul temper, for the duration of our encounter—that

flash of time when we pass him on the street—his "story" will be captured and communicated by his bright yellow tie.

With acquaintances, as opposed to utter strangers, we go beyond the external trappings of clothes, but not entirely. When a close friend who customarily dresses conservatively suddenly appears in garish garb, we are bewildered, confused, sometimes even irrationally angry. We accuse the friend of dressing "out of character." That phrase proves how intimately we believe "character" and clothing are combined: a man of good character dresses one way, we think subconsciously, while a thug necessarily dresses another way. How fervently we trust—or distrust—others is potently influenced by their attire. Sexual attraction is aroused as much by dress as by undress. Clothing *always* colors our reactions. And what we wear *always* colors others' reactions to us.

ABOVE. The impression conveyed by clothing always depends upon the context in which it is viewed. A conventionally outfitted navy blue pin-striped suit is a potent symbol for business rectitude—but who is unaware of the type of business transaction a man in a pin-striped suit has in mind when he's discovered at a massage parlor? And is a man who turns up his collar and flops down on a motorcycle really deeply concerned with business ledgers? Suit: Hart Schaffner & Marx. Case: U.S. Luggage. Model (both images): Jhamil.

MASS TRANSIT

In classical Greek and Roman times, clothing signified status, and only specified colors and embroideries could be worn by respective ranks. During the heyday of the Byzantine Empire, the color purple was reserved exclusively for royal adornment.

Although laws restricting who may wear what are no longer in effect in our supposedly democratic society, clothing is still used as a means of group identification. We see this most clearly in occupations in which literal uniforms are mandated—in the military, in police departments, et cetera. Uniforms help identify the tiered strata of the hierarchy while diminishing any sense of individuality within the same station. In effect, uniforms are purposefully dehumanizing, since their existence announces that the perpetuation of the hierarchy is more important than the nurturing of individuality; nonconformity is a visual and psychological threat to the system.

In restrictive societies, where the parameters of acceptable behavior are strictly and narrowly defined, options in acceptable dress are generally very limited. This is also true of the subgroups within the society. "Peer-group dressing"—when most members of one social group or caste dress in a greatly similar manner—is especially prevalent when "outsiders" are viewed as threatening to the social or moral fabric of the group. By adopting a group "uniform," the group attempts to protect itself from the invasion or infiltration of undesirable "others." Even seemingly harmless deviations from peer-group dressing are perceived as inflammatory, an assault on the status quo. A society marked by rigid conformity in dress is almost always a society in which sexual roles are highly formalized; nonconformists in dress and behavior are in jeopardy of social banishment. In such a milieu, clothing is much more than a body covering; it is also the manifestation of social probity . . . or iniquity.

Conversely, in expansive societies, where sexual and social roles are not rigidly stereotyped and individuality is prized (or at least widely permitted), acceptable modes of dress are diverse and various. This likewise tends to be true of the subgroups within the society as well. Although peer-group dressing may still be evident, great visible variety often exists within each peer group. In fact, the number of socially acceptable peer groups also tends to proliferate, with

BELOW. Clothing appropriateness is not constant but changes with the setting. At vacation spots, for instance, tourists can wear a wide variety of outfits acceptable to the crowd's collective sensibility. Participants in an equestrian event are not given this license. As proof of how deeply notions of appropriate dress are entrenched with territoriality, imagine an exchange of clothing between the two men below and consider the bizarre consequence. Model left, photographed on the Greek island of Mykonos: Lazaro Feleki. Styling by Angelo Droulia. Model right: Richard Smith. Child: Corty Maxfield IV.

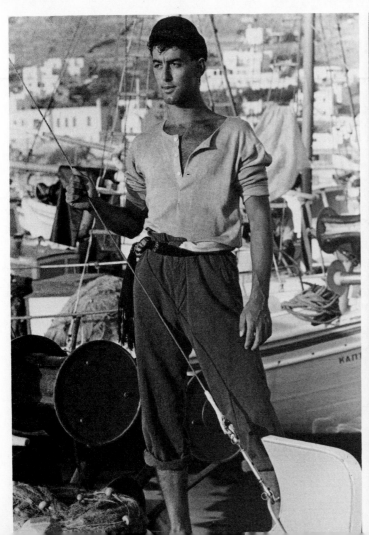

BELOW. Contemporary male attire is often more individualistic than in decades past because a greater variety of styles is now considered acceptable in a greater number of circumstances. Given increased freedom of choice, many men are wearing garb to show off their physiques and to exhibit a free spirit.

Off-duty garb seldom offers any clue about how one makes a living, although more personal information may be transmitted. Any male wearing an outfit like this one openly declares a taste for the theatrical, since the clothing suggests costuming and is self-evidently for "play." Model: Lazaro Feleki. Styling by Angelo Droulia.

the result that the number of modes of attire deemed acceptable (or permissible) also increases. Multiplicity increasingly supersedes conformity in dress as societal prohibitions regarding personal expression and acceptable behavior are relaxed. In such a sphere, although clothing still conveys a sense of etiquette, dress is more significantly a personal tool to convey individual personhood as opposed to communicating societal assignment of rank or role.

Rather than laboring an explanation of how this came to pass, let us find it sufficient to say that men today are receiving far less societal pressure to dress "invisibly"—that is, to dress only in a style so interchangeably similar to that of their peers that individual males visually recede into such a mass of sartorial familiarity that they become virtually invisible, indistinguishable one from another. For decades, American males had been indoctrinated into wearing what were essentially anonymous uniforms.

In years not too distant, if a man wanted to dress "right," he pulled together a basic wardrobe consisting of a navy blazer, a suit of gray flannel and another of pin-striped blue, plus an assortment of oxford-cloth shirts and silk rep ties—the components of the accepted business uniform in the corporate-success-oriented mode. With these, his wardrobe needs were considered fulfilled.

Society is finally allowing men a new visibility, the opportunity to emerge from the anonymous crowd. This sanction reflects the fact that society's view of acceptable male behavior is broader, less limiting, than it has ever been in this century. New concepts—and images—of maleness are emerging. To take full advantage of this enriched social climate, many men must learn new techniques in outfitting themselves. The desired end is not to look "fashionable." The goal is for men to use clothing as a tool for self-expression, even self-discovery.

INSIDE OUT

Although the subject of male attire is commonly referred to as "men's fashion," the semantic implications are too narrow. In most people's minds, the word "fashion" is associated with fads, short-term modes of the moment that probably will not withstand the test of time. To be "in fashion," one must wear outfits that are recognizably current but not yet widely adopted by the populace at large. Fashion magazines are the arbiters of what is "fashionable" garb and what isn't. Trend-spotting is the most important function of fashion magazines, so that their readers can know in advance what is to become fashionable and thereby know in advance how to dress in a "trendy" manner. One season, the "in" look may be suave Italianate styling; the next year's "in" look may be robust Americana. And fashion's wheels revolve. As soon as an "in" look is embraced for mass consumption, it is definitely on its way out, since to be "in fashion," you have to be ahead of the pack. Sometimes several "in" looks emerge—and disappear—simultaneously, since "fashion" is an evolutionary process. Only full-time students of "fashion" can keep track.

Society places little premium on a man's dressing fashionably. To be dressed properly and appropriately is the surer way to win social approval. Neither we nor the garments we wear exist in an unpeopled void. The etiquette of dress is basically divided into two spheres—"on-duty" (business) situations and "off-duty" (leisure or social) contexts. To be dressed fashionably as well as appropriately for specific events may be considered a bonus (and sometimes a handicap), but the main emphasis is always on wearing outfits "proper" to the circumstances . . . if you're courting the attending crowd's approval. However, you mustn't forget that there are several crowds, and inclusion in one may mean exclusion from another. When it comes to dressing, you can't please all of the people all of the time.

Dressing "stylishly" is not the same thing as dressing fashionably. To dress "with style," it is not essential that the outfit be "in" or "trendy." A person possessing "style" wears clothing in a manner considered unconventional by society's homogeneous standards. However, the clothing is worn with such flair—with what appears to be an instinctive expression of the individual's unique personality— that a stylish person wins respect instead of disapproval. When someone with style dresses in a very exaggerated manner, the result may appear idiosyncratic. This is not necessarily bad, provided the individual has the strength of personality to carry off what otherwise might be interpreted—and condemned—as excess. Few men, for example, have enough "style" to wear voluminous fur capes or floppy, flowery bow ties.

On the other hand, although only the rare individual can adapt an idiosyncratic wardrobe style, palatable style—dressing somewhat unconventionally but with controlled excess—is available to every man, since greater latitude is allowed men today in their appearance.

RANK AND FILE

Although men currently enjoy the right to increased expressiveness in their attire, this right does not amount to license. The more structured an event, the greater the expectation of the crowd that those participating in or attending it will wear "proper" clothing. Usually, when high value is placed on an event, the dress expectations are more stringent than for an occasion of less relative significance. Since attending church is viewed as pious, the high value placed on this act explains why wearing appropriate garb is considered very important. Attending a rock concert has none of the time-institutionalized importance of attending Mass. Consequently, "proper"—relatively formal—dress is not deemed nearly as necessary, or even desirable, at a rock concert.

Despite the sociological changes resulting from the feminist movement, high priority is still accorded the man-as-breadwinner syndrome. People may no longer believe that a man's *sole* function is to provide materially for his own, but tremendous value is still assigned to a man's ability to earn wages, to advance occupationally. Depending upon the status of a man's work, there may or may not be unwritten but powerful expectations placed on what he wears. Since little status is attributed to working on a factory assembly line, there is little demand (beyond safety requirements) for a factory worker to wear "proper" clothing. However, greater status is accorded lawyers, and clothing expectations are likewise much greater. Generally, when more elevated status is associated with a profession, greater formality in dress is expected. When a man in a high-status profession breaks the mold and dresses in an extremely informal manner, the societal response is much more critical than when a person in a lesser-ranked job does the same. The practical consequence is that there remains less freedom of personal expression in "on-duty" garb where suits and ties are seen as *de rigueur*.

Some work is high-paying but still lacking in traditional status. "Creative" fields are in this vague terrain. At base, our society is a

ABOVE. A man's occupation highly influences the style of clothing he wears to work—his on-duty garb. Certain professional fields—advertising, architecture, the arts—are seen as more "creative" than law, investing and "businessy" businesses. The staid professions are more highly ranked in our society than creative fields. In highly ranked professions, greater emphasis is placed on dressing in more formal modes, while greater freedom of expression is allowed—in fact, expected—in creative endeavors.

Here, the jauntiness of the outfit slots it as a creative style that a hard-nosed businessman could wear, but with a high risk of receiving disapproval from some of his business associates. Fair? Not at all, but it's impossible to isolate clothing from others' expectations and reactions. Outfit: Pinky & Diane. Model: Mark Richardson.

sexist one, with the power base still fairly male-dominated. Creativity is associated with emotionalism, and emotionalism is thought of as a womanly trait. Because less value is assigned to women than to men, "creative" work lacks the status of the supposedly more objec-tive, hard-nosed business of business. As a result, men working in creative endeavors are especially free to be more expressively uncon-ventional in their dress than males involved in higher-status enter-prises. An artist who dresses like a businessman often is not thought to be genuinely talented.

In contrast to "on-duty" garb, "off-duty" apparel is less laden with expectations. One's "play" time is one's "free" time, so how a man dresses at his leisure does not interfere with his moneymaking po-tential . . . unless he comes into contact with fellow workers or people who might engage his professional services. When busi-ness and pleasure mix, business expectations take the higher seat— and the higher clothing priority. Even at a company picnic, for in-stance, the chairman of the board is expected to dress more formally than the underlings or than he would when hosting a backyard bar-becue for his suburban pals.

Few of these rules concerning the social etiquette of clothes have ever been formalized, but they are constantly at work. Because of the subliminal mechanics involved, many people do not know why they accept or reject the dress of others, but accept or reject they do. Similarly, many people dress incorrectly—which really means im-properly—because they have failed to plumb the etiquette of clothing deeply enough.

NEUTRALITY

Because clothing is not as simple as choosing what color tie looks attractive with what striped shirt, and because most men lack understanding of why certain clothing combinations elicit certain responses in certain settings, and also because men traditionally have been taught very little about clothing selection, their own dress has been an enigma to many otherwise insightful and incisive males. Subjected to the crosscurrents of conflicting, sometimes mutually exclusive, expectations, many a man has often handled (more precisely, mishandled) his wardrobe by failing to come to grips with it in any artful or beneficial way. The most common mistake has simply been to assemble "basic" pieces that will neither surprise nor offend —so-called "classic" garments in neutral colors and unexceptional fabrications. The reputed virtue of these choices is blandness. Lacking in character, the clothing supposedly serves as a neutral backdrop from which the man himself can step and shine forth. What works in theory does not work in practice.

Since we now know that clothing *always* colors onlookers' reactions, neutral clothing conveys only neutrality, offering no incentive to investigate deeper. The "neutral" man is uncomfortably akin to the neutered man: he appears dehumanized and devoid of spirit or passion. Neutral clothing is but another anonymous uniform, and

RIGHT. When society allows—or when iconoclasts insist upon it, regardless of consequences—clothing becomes a means of expressing individuality. Here is a classic seersucker sport coat worn in a decidedly unclassic way. In today's fairly liberated milieu, such an outfit may be considered terrific, so-so, perhaps strange or shades in between, but wearing this look will only rarely be deemed offensive. In the 1950s, dressing this way would have been unthinkable if you didn't want the neighbors to talk. Shirt: Armand Diradourian. Model: Joshua Tyler Barrett.

uniforms tend to censor the feelings of their wearers, giving the impression that no spontaneous feelings exist beneath the characterless facade. Even within the highly structured territory of high-status professions, some sense of humanity is desirable.

Ironically, too many men still gravitate toward wearing neutral uniforms out of conditioning and unthinking ease. Past concepts of maleness formed the societal base for shrouding men in neutral uniforms. At one time it was felt that men had only one function in life: to be an archetypal Male, defender of the hearth and supplier of the bacon. Whereas women were eminently emotional, men were preeminently objective, universally the same. One uniform could be worn by all because to be a real man meant only one thing: to be the financial provider and distributor. That is why the male wardrobe revolved almost exclusively around the corporate-success-oriented wardrobe.

Today we know that maleness comprises many traits, that being a man means being multidimensional. In fact, we know that selfhood is composed of more than one self: man has his professional self, his private self, even his fantasy self. Likewise, every man is a compilation of various attributes. To be a well-rounded individual, a man will highlight one facet of his personality in certain circumstances and will highlight others at other times. This isn't duplicity; it's part of being a whole person, not a walking-talking stereotype.

The ramifications of a man's being multitudinous are many. Savvy men will delve into the various components of their natures. They will not be confined by outmoded expressions of male behavior. A good beginning in this quest is exploring clothing as a means of self-awareness. Dressing to reveal various personal traits is a sure way of getting in touch with those traits. Dressing the free way is a route to self-expansion.

MOVING ON

The premise of this book is that men need not—in fact, should not—view themselves or their wardrobes statically. Men can—and should—use style to announce the many facets and dimensions of themselves. What this means for you is this: in certain circumstances, you may choose to highlight one attribute visibly (perhaps your sensuality when the time and occasion are right), but you may prefer to showcase another attribute (perhaps your occupational industriousness) in a different situation. If you examine what you want and the social milieu in which you're seeking your goals, you will better be able to enlist clothing to reach your aspirations. By projecting a variety of attributes and characteristics, you expand your horizons. However, don't misunderstand. You should not be using clothing as a way to dupe others. Clothing should not be asked to deceive, disguise or masquerade. Clothing should expose the real you, not present a pretender.

By reading this book, you will understand more about how dressing the free way can make your communication with others more honest and more direct, because clothing will reinforce the many dimensions of your personality. Each chapter will discuss a separate attribute and demonstrate how clothing conveys the appropriate im-

NEAR RIGHT. This outfit speaks very eloquently for itself, with no aid from the nondescript background. Very evidently this is a dressy suit with a great deal of stature. (Double-breasted suit coats almost always convey a sense of authority.) There's not one solid fabric in the outfit; all the pieces come together surely and ingeniously.

Your eyes tell you that this man is not run-of-the-mill . . . and you've never heard him speak a word. Outfit: Alexander Julian. Model (all three shots): Troy Lee Hinkle.

CENTER. Here's the same fellow in a not-so-elegant mood. He's playing peekaboo with his chest, which is downright suggestive. With the shirt sleeves rolled above the elbow, he's exposing yet more flesh. The impression of sensuality can't be overlooked, since it is conveyed in each item he's wearing.

For example, the vest has several highly visible pockets and other details that subliminally open numerous entries to place hands closer to the body. The pants have a relatively short fly . . . facilitating fast unzipping. But the biggest clue is the watch hanging on the vest, subliminally announcing his disregard for strict timetables: he has all the time in the world for a good time. Shirt: Hannes B. Vest: The Trader.

FAR RIGHT. And here he is again, in a more whimsical mood. Since all the colors are relatively pale, the look is vastly less authoritative and less dressy than the suit in the first photo. One look isn't "better" than the other; they simply communicate different traits. Also, they are appropriate in different settings.

This more casual—but nonetheless ingenious—look would be perfectly at ease at a patio brunch, while the double-breasted suit could appear too stuffy. Conversely, the double-breasted suit would be sublime at a midnight sit-down dinner for twelve, while the sport-coat ensemble might come across as overly flip. Still, flipness—and hipness—are at the core of this ensemble's character.

With a different (solid) tie and without the nifty suspenders, the outfit would be acceptable, predictable and unexceptional—uncommunicative; with them, it virtually speaks of fun . . . and the guy still hasn't opened his mouth. Outfit: Garrick Anderson.

agery of that characteristic. The extent to which you adopt these looks will depend upon the etiquette of the situation, what you are seeking and your personality makeup.

Don't fall into the trap of asking for a "basic" wardrobe to help you project all these traits. As you learned when thinking about clothing as a neutral backdrop, putting together one set of garments to cover all possibilities just doesn't work, and it's a pitfall. You must take some responsibility for yourself. You must decide what is most meaningful to you and then dress accordingly. You must also decide how roughly you want to rock society's boat. You can dive more swimmingly and expressively into the waters of off-duty apparel than you can into the work pool of on-duty garb. But you don't need to

make a huge splash to dress in the free way. This book will show you small strokes that can help you cover a lot of distance in meaningfully transforming your dress.

Another reward will also be yours. Right now, by accident you may be misinforming others about yourself simply because you're dressing thoughtlessly, with no purposeful objective. After investigating the imagery of clothes, you can correct any faulty messages you've been innocently transmitting. That's the ultimate advantage in dressing the free way: you're free to be on your way with the secure knowledge that you're telling others what you want them to hear about you. You control the truth and accuracy of the message because *you* are the real message.

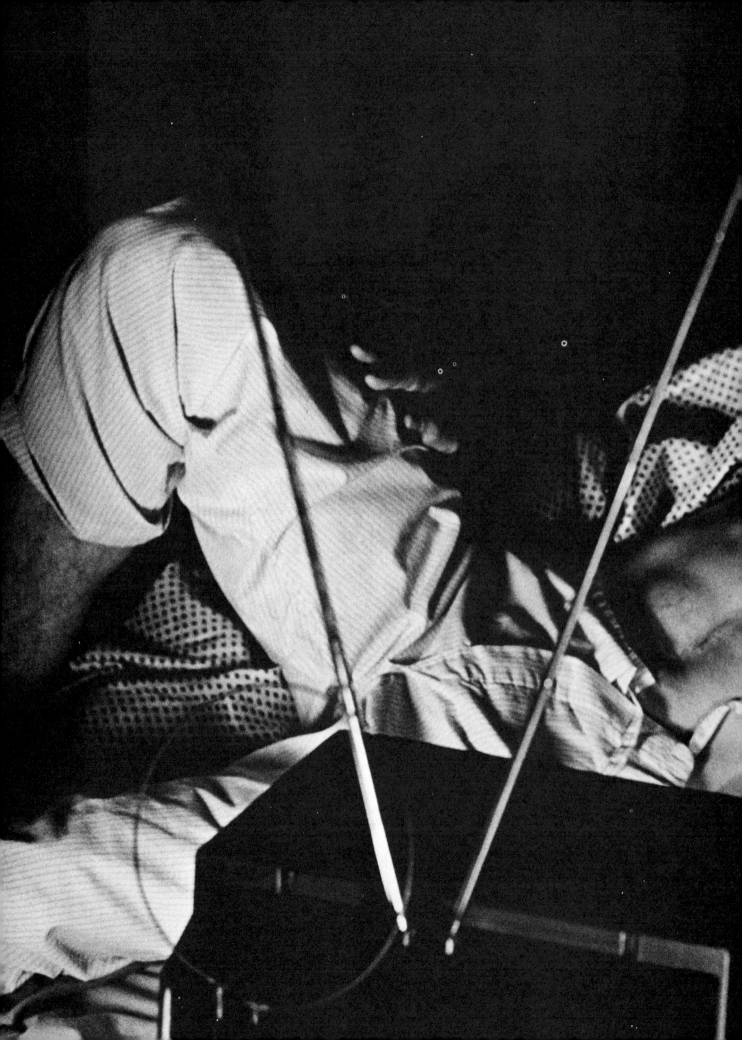

PART I
OFF-DUTY GARB

CHAPTER 1
SEXY!

BODY COVERINGS

Get set. If you're unwilling to view yourself from a new angle, you're not ready for this chapter.

For starters, you must take an imaginary flight outside yourself. Picture the embodiment of all your erotic fantasies. Now, step inside the mind of this epitome of desirability. Look at yourself through that wondrous person's eyes. On the basis of your appearance alone, would your dreamed-of lover choose you as an ideal mate?

Before collapsing in despair, recognize that the purpose of this exercise is not to humble you. The real lesson to be learned is that many others look at you the same way you look at many of them—with sex in mind.

What we're talking about is sexual attraction. You know you're susceptible to it. Just don't forget that others are too. Since you experience no difficulty in gazing upon strangers and sizing them up physically, don't balk at the notion that strangers size you up as well. Also, don't forget that many strangers are walking around out there to whom you don't respond with burning eroticism. Many strangers may not be responding to you that way either . . . even though you wish they would. Sexual attraction, alas, isn't always reciprocated.

In recent years, many sexual stereotypes have bit the dust. Women and minorities have asserted themselves, forcing society to reexamine its values. The feminist movement has taught attuned men that it no longer pays to be chauvinistic oafs. The gay movement has taught receptive men that macho braggadocio isn't sublime. The ongoing civil rights movement has taught empathetic individuals that a history of abuse is no justification for injustice. Various movements have combined to redefine sexual and social attitudes, with

PRECEDING DOUBLE-PAGE SPREAD. The epitome of off-duty garb is sleepwear, which only extremely intimate acquaintances ever glimpse you in. Off-duty garb is much more personally expressive—and can consequently be much sexier—than the on-duty garb which your co-workers see you wearing. Robe & pj bottoms: Ron Chereskin. Model: Brian Terrell.

LEFT. Sexy clothing covers a wide gamut of expressions, but the intent is always to highlight the body's sensuality. The better the physique, the sexier the impression, since relatively few people go off into flights of fancy without sensory provocation. Of course, what represents the most attractive male body is relative. So is the question of how much of the body can be bared to strangers.

Deliberate titillation can sometimes be a turn-off, but clothing that acts as a turn-on helps set the stage for disrobing when the time is right. Model: John Burke.

the consequence that the entrenched notion that white middle-class males are supreme has been successfully challenged at last.

When the concentration of power is wrested from one sole group and apportioned into the hands of many, the possession of limited power is not enough to ensure great status or desirability. With men wielding less absolute (if still superior) power, today a new emphasis has been placed on physical as well as economic desirability, since simply being male doesn't make any and every man, whatever the specimen, automatically and necessarily a great catch. Today's sought-after male must have something extra other than his gender. In courtship, often that extra is sex appeal. Even a terrific personality or great wealth may not win the day . . . or the mate.

You are more, of course, than a sexual object, just as a woman is. But if you ignore your own potential for sexual magnetism, no one else may fall under its sway. For better or worse—one hopes, better —we all have bodies as well as minds and emotions. Physical attributes are the core of physical attraction. Physical attraction may blossom into a world-shaking love affair, even a divorceproof marriage— or it may fizzle. Whatever the ultimate outcome, when strangers first meet, physical evaluation precedes all else. Clothing helps set the scene for the scenario that is to be acted out in the human drama. You doubt this? Why do movie producers employ costume designers? So that we viewers can subconsciously place the players correctly in their roles. When we put on our clothes, we are our own costume designers. If we're adept, we can augment our appeal. If we're inept, we can diminish it. Don't flub it.

PICTURE FRAMES

You're rushing much, much too fast if you think of your clothes as only something to remove—an encumbrance—before you can get down to erotic business. The right clothes can enhance your sexual magnetism. They won't improve your sexual virtuosity; they *will* make you appear more sensual . . . until the payoff comes. Then it's up to you, your equipment and your technique.

Sexy clothes are basically body-conscious garments which accentuate what is unique about the male physique and which underplay what is not distinctively and anatomically "masculine." (The one exception is male genitalia; except in the gay world, flagrantly flaunting one's crotch is considered off-puttingly vulgar, not sexy.)

Perhaps ironically, the trappings of homosexual attraction aren't fundamentally at odds with the vestments of heterosexual attraction; at first sighting, before words are exchanged and an evaluation of personality takes place, it is generally attractive "maleness" that appeals to both a heterosexual female and a homosexual male. Consequently, a fellow doesn't dress "straight" or "gay." When you dress to project a sexy aura, of whatever variety, you dress to make the most of your male physique.

Body-conscious clothing comes in different degrees. Swimming trunks are more revealing than jeans, but not automatically sexier. *Where* you wear what clothes makes all the difference. Wearing a bikini to the opera isn't sexy; it's scandalous. Wearing white tie and tails to the beach isn't sexy or scandalous; it's ludicrous. Neither bikini nor white tie is appropriate for washing clothes at the Laundromat. Jeans are. At the Laundromat, jeans can be sexy because they're right for the occasion. But if you wear sexy jeans to the opera, you'll probably be frowned upon. Although some formal clothing projects a degree of sex appeal, clothing that's too sexy can be too much for certain circumstances. On-duty garb should seldom be overtly sexy, since sex and work don't mix (or so the age-old theory goes), so only marginally sexy clothes are ever okay in the business milieu. Off-duty garb can send out sexy signals more strongly and entail less fear of censure.

LEFT. A bare chest is overtly sexy. So is a pair of jeans left unbuttoned at the waist. While this minimal outfit appears innocently sexy at the clothesline, it would not travel well to a restaurant. Model: Todd Bentley.

BELOW. Exposing large amounts of skin is more permissible at a vacation resort than at a PTA meeting. When very abbreviated attire is customary—for instance, for basking in the sun—sometimes it is sexier not to bare the maximum.

A pair of shorts rolled up the thighs appears sexier than a bikini because they suggest you have given in to an irresistible hedonistic urge. Spontaneity is sexier than a heavy-handed attempt to look sexy. Model: Les Lyden.

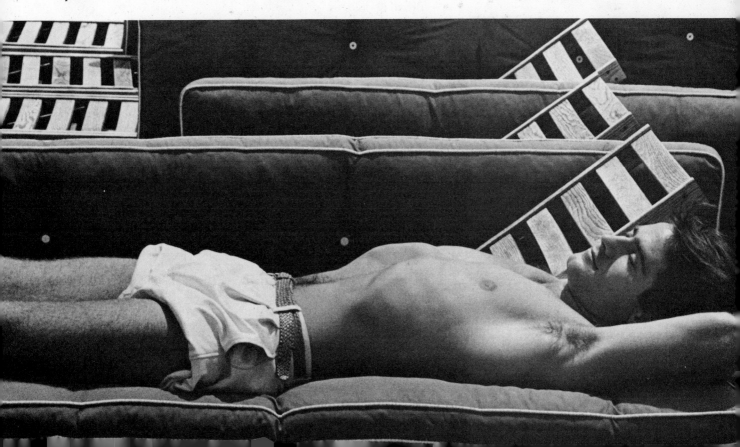

Obviously, if your body isn't worth cheering about, you can't hope to elicit the same physical and emotional response as a guy with a worked-out frame. Although you're ahead with a well-proportioned build, you don't need to look like an Olympic athlete. A reasonably toned body beneath body-conscious clothing will still look better than a decathlon-winning physique obscured by unflattering garb. On the other hand, body-conscious clothing on unappealing frames —ones greatly either over- or underweight—compound any imperfections. Sexy clothing on unsexy bodies can lead to ridicule. If you've got it, flaunt it. If not, maybe you should pass . . . until your body does have the tone.

LETTER PERFECT

Several studies have shown that a majority of women find the most erotic component of a man's body his buttocks. After buns, a man's chest is usually singled out as the sexiest part of his body. Women's behinds and chests are very, very different from men's, and they are also generally considered the sexiest parts of women's bodies as well. Ankles or ears are not so greatly different from sex to sex, which is why ankles and ears are less often the stuff of fantasy. In terms of perceived sexual attraction and attractiveness, long live the differences between the sexes.

Culturally, we now realize that the boundaries of so-called masculine and feminine behavior are much broader than we once thought. Such relativity doesn't extend to our perceptions of anatomy. Almost universally, the *femaleness* of the female body and the *maleness* of the male body win admiration. (That difference also happens to affect the birthrate.)

As a man, then, you want your clothing to accentuate those parts of your body which are most "male." Although sexual fantasies are highly individualistic (and sometimes fetishistic), here is a list of the prized "male" physical attributes:

- Robust neck.
- Broad shoulders.
- Expansive chest.
- Strong biceps.
- Firm waistline.
- Flat abdomen.
- Narrow hips.
- Tight buttocks.
- Developed thighs.

(Genitals aren't listed because they're generally too private to be public.)

Obviously, the only way to display all these assets all the time is to dress only in an array of G-string pouches. That will not meet with general approval. To dress sexily—that is, to dress to accentuate your maleness—you should be selective and somewhat subtle. Circumstances will dictate how discreet you will or won't be. For the moment, just mull over the implications of the list. "Athleticism" is the body imagery most associated with physical magnetism. In today's milieu, being physically attractive is equated with appearing physically fit.

Letters of the alphabet can be assigned to designate the body configurations regarded as attractively and athletically "male."

V. Massive shoulders are symbolically male. Wide shoulders

BELOW. An athletically defined body epitomizes the current ideal of sexiness. In fact, sport clothing of most types helps generate sexual appeal. Turning down the elasticized waistband on gym shorts is subliminally erotic, allowing a glimpse of what's usually hidden, implying that more than meets the eye is yet to come. Model: Brian Terrell.

RIGHT. During Victorian times, it was considered impolite even to allude to the fact that people coupled. Today some folk are still squeamish about discussing sex and are not totally at ease viewing the male body, although these same people experience far less difficulty looking at the unadorned female form. In particular, certain males (especially those who haven't caught up with the times—of whom, unfortunately, the numbers are many) will slur their fellows who are unabashed about presenting themselves in a sexy light.

So what? The aim of sexy clothing is to arouse the right partners, excluding prudes, bigots and the narrow-minded. If you have the potential to look like a sun god in swimwear, go for it. Bathing briefs: Speedo. Model: Robert Henry.

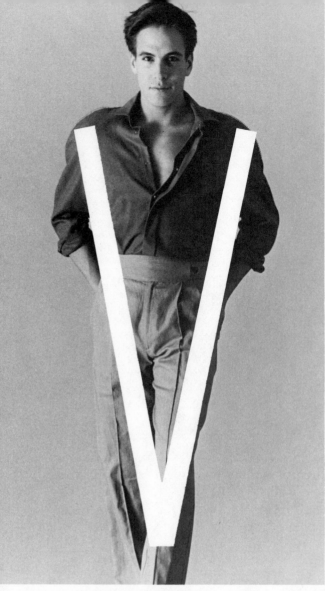

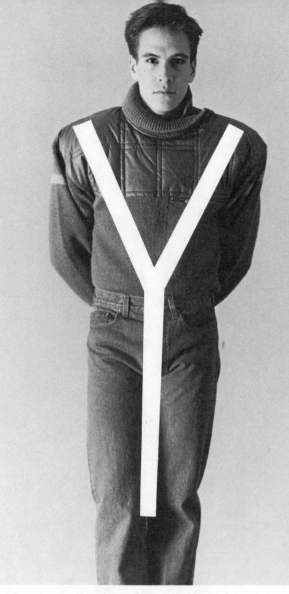

LEFT. The V shape is sexy because it emphasizes the power of the male torso. The barely visible tiny zipper teeth outlining the top of the shoulders and running down the arms of the shirt sleeves might appear to be only whimsical decoration, but they also make the shoulders and arms appear more massive. (A strategic stripe would do the same.)

Leaving the top shirt buttons unbuttoned creates an actual V of exposed flesh. Tucking in the shirt makes the chest appear more V-like. The tapered, slightly pegged trousers likewise reinforce the overall V shape.

Here, the color tones of the shirt and pants are fairly similar. This relative lack of contrast makes the V impression more fluid than if the garments were in markedly different shades. Model (for all three photographs): Michael Hart.

CENTER. The Y outline is also sexy. Even greater emphasis is afforded the shoulders and chest here because the trousers are tight. The quilting on the yoke magnifies the chest. The colorful knit bands create an optical illusion of wider, stronger shoulders. All stylistic flourishes augment the upper-body proportions. The faded jeans are snug enough to suggest all the body parts beneath without truly exposing them.

above narrow hips reinforce physiological maleness. The idealized male torso is V-shaped, tapering in almost straight converging lines from the shoulders' width to a point below the pelvis, giving prominent importance to the chest. Clothing that maintains the image of a V-shaped torso is therefore more fundamentally masculine—and sexy—than clothing that doesn't. The appeal of V-shaped clothing is that it corresponds to the supposed natural flow of the male physique. Although the body itself is not clearly outlined (as it would be in body-clinging garb), there is a sense of the body's being almost visible as it moves beneath the clothing.

RIGHT. *The T is the third sexy clothing configuration, although it demands a very good body, since so little is left to the imagination. This is no optical illusion: what you see is what the wearer's body is, since this degree of tightness is highly revealing.*

Because the sweater and pants are both dark, the T impression is more apparent than if they were in contrasting tones.

Y. If you consider the entire male body, you can think of it as Y-shaped. Viewed in this way, the torso is still a V. The addition of legs adds a "tail" to the V, making a Y. The configuration is more dramatically "male" than the V-shaped body because the brawn and bulk of the male chest are accented even more. So is the male butt. Relatively roomy tops—or relatively tight tops over a chest that's emphatic in its own right—worn with tight, narrow-legged bottoms that hug a man's hips add to a Y-shaped impression.

T. Picture a man with his arms extended to the sides (palms down) at shoulder height. If you overlook his head, he resembles the letter T. T-shaped clothing is the most radically male type of attire, since it presents the male most explicitly. Its sexiness depends upon the sexiness of the body wearing it.

Letters can also be assigned to body configurations *not* considered attractively or athletically male.

X. A wasplike waist is not male. An X-shaped body is too reminiscent of a female hourglass form. Voluminous tops and bottoms, cinched at the waist, aren't sexually appealing male attire.

H. Uniform shapelessness isn't sexy either. Although few men are truly H-shaped, even a man with a superb build can appear H-shaped in a large, sacklike suit. When all body contours are lost inside shapeless attire, you don't hear sighs of approval or lust.

O. This is the shape of an overweight man. The softness of a bulky body diminishes maleness, transforming the physique into androgynous neuterdom. Any clothing on an O-shaped body automatically becomes O-shaped apparel despite itself.

I. This is the shape of an underweight man. The stringiness of a thin body also diminishes maleness, though not as drastically as an overweight frame. Suit jackets with padded shoulders, for instance, can help an I-shaped body look T-shaped. Unhappily, an I-shaped body in swim trunks will always look I-shaped, and you can't find T-shirts with padded shoulders.

Since the V, Y and T configurations all impart sex appeal, and since each configuration can be assembled in countless ways, various are the means to project heightened sensuality. Of course, there are many gradations in sexy attire, too. But without exception, for an outfit to be sexy it must flatter the physique one way or another. With forethought, you can increase your physical magnetism in almost every type of garb—but not if the clothing fails to idealize your "maleness."

CHANGEABLE PARTS

Although some folks with idiosyncratic penchants will disagree, no article of clothing is intrinsically sexy when no one is wearing it. In a dresser drawer, even the skimpiest underclothing isn't truly erotic. Put that skimpy underclothing on an attractive body: then we're talking about something else.

In short, clothing is not clothing is not clothing. Clothing is a series of garments of no practical consequence until worn. The visual relationship with the wearer's body determines how sexy attire is or isn't.

Whenever you appear in public, generally you wear an outfit made up of several articles of clothing. How congruous these articles are, and how effectively *all* the garments combine to project a single characteristic, determine how potently you make the impression you intend.

When a man wears sexy pants, a sexy shirt and a sexy pair of shoes, all else being equal, he'll appear sexier than a man wearing sexy pants with an ill-fitting, oversized shirt and a pair of business wing-tips. In fact, despite the sexy pants, the latter man probably won't seem sexy at all, since the other components of his outfit are transmitting nonsexy, contradictory signals. This man will be perceived as a thoughtless, sloppy dresser with his feet rooted in business concerns even when he's supposedly having fun. His outfit tells viewers that he's completely lacking in sartorial talent, and that probably he's a boob.

When components are so contradictory as to become incongruous, the message received is bizarre. Even at Atlantic City, when a man wears business shoes and socks with swim trunks, the look he presents is outré . . . as bizarre as a man would look in a vested suit gliding along the Boardwalk on roller skates. Several very incongruous combinations of clothing in very different moods suggest dementia. Think of the impression that shopping-bag ladies create as they shuffle down the street.

A less extreme example: a man wearing sexy pants with an ordinary plaid sport shirt and a typical pair of jogging shoes. He *may* appear somewhat sexy . . . or ordinary . . . or sporty. The combined components of his outfit are not strongly contradictory or incongruous. But they aren't very communicative either. If the man wore a sexy shirt with the sexy pants but left on the jogging shoes, his outfit would be more expressive and he would appear more expressly sexy. But to convey sensuality most strongly, he would be better off in sexy, not typical jogging, shoes, and sexy everything else.

But sometimes juxtapositions are sexy, as when a garment usually associated with one setting is worn within another. Someone wearing gym togs jogging along Wall Street will look sexier, if his clothes and body are sexy, than he will when he's running in a marathon, because in the latter setting he will be surrounded by other runners similarly attired. Yet the same man, clad in the same jogging outfit, would not look sexy in a Wall Street board meeting; he would look incongruous. Juxtaposition works, but only within limits.

BODY POLITIC

Individual garments convey attributes in a number of ways, and not all garments convey only one attribute. The most important variables are the shape, the texture and the color and/or pattern of the garments. Many garments also communicate their own inherent psychology. Read the following discussion carefully, since these variables affect the projection of other characteristics as well as sex appeal.

SHAPE

As you know, the overall shape of an outfit is instrumental in its impression, with V-, Y- and T-shapes considered the most attractively "male." But individual garments have their own shapes, so they either contribute to or detract from the outfit's overall configuration.

The shape of a garment is usually referred to as its cut. Pants, for instance, may be cut to be straight-legged, or pegged, or in a variety of ways. Shirts may be cut to be form-fitting, or straight from the armholes to the tail, or roomy, or in other ways too. Sweaters can be tight or baggy, long or short, or in between. How garments are cut

NEAR RIGHT. Unlike the other outfit on the page, this one has little stylistic panache. In fact, it makes an anti-fashion statement because it could be the work garb of a manual laborer. No concession is made to looking "done up." That lack of concession is one reason some will find the outfit sexy (while others may consider it simply sloppy). Yet the ensemble has no false pretensions, no false airs.

It does have a sense of humor in the T-shirt with the figure flexing its muscle. The purposefully oversized T-shirt proves the guy doesn't take himself too seriously and thereby makes the tightness of the jeans appear less "animal."

On the subliminal level, catching sight of the strap of the undershirt moves an onlooker's eyes toward the torso. The layers of hooded sweat shirt and sleeveless vest bring to mind qualities of a sexy vagabond. This is the outfit of someone with street smarts. Model: Jimmy Nickerson.

FAR RIGHT. Since there are many ways to convey sexiness, but not an infinity of circumstances where projecting sexiness is appropriate, you must consider the social milieu when selecting your garb. Wherever people meet to dance, for instance, the unwritten code is to dress freely: discos are among the few public places left where limited exhibitionism is tolerated. This outfit, drenched in sexuality, is not recommended for the symphony.

Unless they are part of a sport ensemble, tank tops, whether roomy like this one or skin-tight, should be worn only where the crowd is very relaxed. Here, the unusual leather belt is self-evidently for adornment, not to hold the pants up. Its size makes a sizable impression, calling attention to its decorative purpose.

In most primitive cultures, male self-adornment is part of the courtship ritual. When rhythmic music is in the air, we respond primitively and most forms of male self-adornment, perhaps incongruous in other settings, tend to be perceived as sexy. Top & pants: Bech Thomassen. Belt: Robin Khan. Model: Jhamil. Photographed at Times Square, New York City.

LEFT. *Here is another example of "street clothes" (with high-fashion price tags) that are sexy.*

The roomy proportions of the leather jacket combined with the snug jeans create the sexy Y shape. But the outfit has more going for it than merely that.

The jacket's plushly lined hood and the hand-loomed textural scarf tell onlookers that this man responds to the soft touch. The body of the grained leather jacket has several zippered openings and buttoned flaps, suggesting hidden treasures to be discovered beneath the jacket . . . if a stranger's hands could penetrate.

Although complete with its own belt, the jacket remains unfastened, an open invitation, implying that disrobing has already begun. The snug denim jeans, softened by repeated washing, move freely with the body and don't present an off-putting facade. Jacket: Giorgio Armani. Scarf: Susan Horton. Model (also in the inset): Doug Spitz.

INSET. *Now, another sexy look. This time the fellow wears a T-shirt vaguely akin to an athletic jersey. ("Competition" is one of the words running illegibly across the yoke.) The top lettering optically widens the shoulders, and rolling up the sleeves draws attention to the biceps.*

Colored in brilliant hues, the shirt is eye-catching, and catching the eye of the beholder is sexy strategy. The clamdiggers expose the calf and reinforce the fact that hunks don't shave their legs. T-shirt: Enrico Coveri. Clamdiggers: Float.

affects their proportions, and differently proportioned garments in various combinations transmit different traits.

For example, pants that are cut to accent the behind are always sexier than pants that aren't. Pants that are roomy in the thighs but proportionately narrower in the knee and cuff can still be cut to accent the contours of the backside, so they are not less or more sexy than butt-clinging jeans, only sexy in different ways. By contrast, straight-legged pants with ample room in the behind are never sexy in themselves. But if they are worn with a bulky sweater that does not extend much lower than the waist, the combined garments give a sexier (Y-shaped) impression than if the straight-legged, roomy-in-the-behind pants are worn with a drooping cardigan sweater (imparting an H-shape). Much sexier would be the bulky, not-too-low-at-the-waist sweater worn with the roomy-in-the-thigh, butt-accenting trousers (making a V-shaped impression). Equally sexy would be the same sweater worn with butt-clinging jeans (for a more emphatic Y-shape) . . . provided the colors and textures of one outfit are no more or less sexy than those of the other.

The individual shape of garments, then, is important, but not as significant as the overall impression made by the combination of shapes. And texture and color can't be forgotten. Yet one must also remember that combinations ineffectual in projecting one trait may effectively convey another. Although the cardigan-and-straight-legged-pants combination is less sexy than the others, it is also more friendly than the others.

Shortly we'll be discussing various categories of clothing to pinpoint individual items that are sexier than others; but don't forget that shape is only one ingredient, and that shapes must combine in particular ways for optimal results.

TEXTURE

When we cover our skin with clothes, the garb's fabrics become our skin replacement, our "second skin." Vinyl is a thick, hard fabric that covers the body like armor. It connotes negative desire, a standoffishness, a don't-touch-me attitude. As a result, vinyl clothing—such as a foul-weather slicker—is anything but sexy.

Greatly affecting the sexiness of clothing is its texture. More tactile textures—ones subliminally inviting others to touch the fabric (the skin substitute)—have more underlying sex appeal than thick, hard textures. Cashmere, mohair and other soft, luxurious fabrics that feel warm to the touch are thus very sexy. Before it has been softened by repeated wearings, denim is a strong, durable fabric that is too stiff and forbidding to be sexy. However, denim ages well, becoming more sexy with the passage of time; it then relaxes on the body, becoming body-conscious gear.

Leather is slightly problematical. Thick black leather can connote violence, the phantasmagoria of sadomasochism. However, when leather is worn with less threatening textures, it can convey a certain sexiness—the sexiness of controlled danger, the excitement of a sexual dare that is essentially safe. Soft leathers (commonly called glove leathers even when made into pants) are generally sexier than the thick, hard leathers that conjure up motorcycle gangs.

Soft leathers exhibit more "drape" than hard ones. In clothing parlance, drape refers to the way a fabric rests on the body. Stiff fabrics have little drape; they encase the body, limiting visible movement of the body parts. Fabrics that drape loosely on the body emphasize body parts more strongly, moving more freely with the body and thereby increasing physical awareness. For these reasons likewise

RIGHT. When we cover our skin with clothing, the various fabrics of the apparel become our skin substitutes. Soft textures stir a stronger desire within onlookers to touch them than slick, hard ones do, so fabrics strong on tactility offer the stronger come-on.

But sometimes our eyes fool us. Take a look at this sport coat. It is extremely tactile, right? Wrong. It only seems so. The pattern creates an optical illusion of textural depth although the weave is basically on the flat side.

When our senses deceive us, we respond to the deception, not to the reality. Thus, although this jacket

isn't truly tactile, onlookers will react to it as if it were.

The leather pants are also up to a slight deception. A stripe has been pressed upon them, thereby lessening the hardness of their impression and actually making the pants more supple . . . and more sensual, less "leather-boyish," even though, when all is said and done, they remain leather pants.

The juxtaposition of the formal shirt, the leather pants and the slouchy sport coat is handsomely original and helps convey sexiness. *Outfit: Andrew Fezza. Model: John Sommi.*

soft leathers are sexier than hard ones, except for people with very specialized tastes.

Like leathers, suedes are animal in origin and project some animalism. Also like leathers, suedes in excess in one outfit can appear too costumed, a parody of sexual appeal. On the other hand, a garment made of soft suede can exude a different sort of sexiness than one of soft leather. Soft suedes project less of an aura of the enticing taboo. With their brushed surfaces, suedes are tactilely more inviting than leathers. Their touch-me textures account for their appeal.

Some fabrics are ambivalently sexy. Lacy, gauzy textures are so intimately entrenched in the imagery of female sexuality that they seldom if ever appear sexy when worn by men. Chiffon also fits into this category. To a lesser degree, the same can be said of silks and satins that drape sensuously on women but sometimes incongruously on men. Silk garments can, in certain instances, be sexy, though an element of risk is involved in wearing them, since to some they may be a turn-off. Wearing velvets and velours courts the same risk. In general, for a man to successfully—and sexily—wear fabrics

or textures strongly associated with female sexuality, the fabrics or textures must be harder than those women wear. Silk trousers, for instance, can be very sexy, provided they're of a heavy weight that's thicker than a woman's filmy silk blouse.

Certain textures are fairly neutral in their sexuality. The flannels found in men's suits, for instance, cannot be classified as particularly sexy or not. However, flannels are slightly more sexy than gabardines, which possess a flatter, harder surface. Flannel has a napped, brushed surface, so it is warmer to the eye and to the touch. In a similar vein, tweeds are not especially sexy in and of themselves. But they project an earthiness that is often integral to sexuality. Compared with twills—very stout, hardy fabrics with definite diagonal cords—tweeds are the sexier of the two . . . except when twill garments are cut in a somewhat military manner. There is still a sexual aura surrounding military-derived styling, provided the style doesn't become so overstated as to suggest an urban guerrilla or a man with a Storm Trooper fixation.

But although, in this fast survey, some textures are shown to be inherently sexier than others, what really counts is still how all the ingredients in an outfit work together. And it mustn't be forgotten that outfits which appear to be sexy in one setting may be thought outrageous in another.

COLOR

Color is arguably the most important variable in men's garb. Certainly it is very, very potent. Take the color red. Physiologically, it induces a quickening of our heartbeat when we view it. No wonder it is linked to passion. Or take the color blue. It is so restful to our eyes that physiologically it slows down our heartbeat, calming us. Serene blue is allied with reserve, not sexuality.

Our reactions to colors are deeply ingrained and often hard to alter. Certain colors are united in our subconsciousness with the female gender. Pink is one. Lavender is another. That is not to say that men do not wear pink or lavender. Nor is there a suggestion that a man wearing pink or lavender is automatically seen as effeminate. What is true is that whenever a man wears pink or lavender he will be singled out more swiftly than a man attired in blue, a color traditionally associated with the male gender, even though women also wear it. The message is simple: any color that is not strongly and fundamentally associated with maleness will grab attention when a man wears it. This can be good or bad. Certainly sexual attraction hinges on being noticed, on projecting some quality or qualities other men lack by comparison. On the other hand, if that projected aura is too lacking in maleness, dismay may supplant attraction.

The colors most commonly worn by men are blue, brown, gray and green—mainly cool or neutral, emotionally "objective" colors. (So-called "feminine" colors are mostly warm and "subjective.") While "masculine" colors do reinforce maleness, they can also appear more commonplace than untraditional color combinations. The knack in enlisting color to convey sex appeal is generally to wear enough male hues to ensure that the outfit has a male anchor, yet to wear some shades that are intriguing enough to provoke interest.

But color isn't separated from pattern. (Even solid colors can be thought of as patterned when they're combined with other solid colors, since the combinations create patterns of color blocks.) Florals are so fundamentally attached to our notions of female patterns that even if floral-patterned trousers are colored in male hues, the trousers are still perceived as more womanly than manly.

ABOVE. *While the athleticism of this tank top is very sexy when worn by someone with strong musculature, color likewise adds to or detracts from a sexy impression. Impossible to discern in a black-and-white photograph, this top is pale yellow—a "warm" color conveying more warm sensuality than pure white.*

The striped shorts impart sexiness too, because of the way the straight up-and-down verticality of the pattern is altered by the human body inside: as the man runs, the stripes curve here and there to accommodate the contours of the behind, the thighs, the entire mobile apparatus. Thus, the mutable striping makes observers more aware of the moving body inside the shorts than if they were one solid color. Tank top & shorts: Float. Model. Peter Macci.

On the other hand, plaids, though not exclusively manly, have a much stronger male identification than florals. When plaid garments are cut in a decidedly manly way but are colored in hues not necessarily thought of as manly colors, the result is more attention-getting than that of a similar plaid garment colored in only so-called manly colors.

Vivid colors (and patterns) are visually (and physiologically) more exciting than drab colors, so they project greater sex appeal, if the combinations aren't so vivid as to be garish or flamboyant. Per usual, what is vividly exciting in one milieu may be extravagantly flamboyant in another. A jade green sport coat is acceptable for dancing at the country club but not for mourning a relative at a funeral. *Where an outfit is worn always determines its propriety.*

Pastel colors, less intense than primary ones because pastels lose their intensity with the infusion of white, do not make as loud a statement as vivid colors. However, they are not really unsexy, because they convey a soft warmth. Their sexiness isn't of the pyrotechnic variety; pastels are more cuddly, huggable.

Offbeat colors (and patterns) convey unconventional tastes. Offbeat colors, then, may not be a turn-on to those unfortunates who see sex solely as a means of procreation, but they can be tantalizing to those more dedicated to the joys and wonders of fleshly experimentation.

But even the sexually unadventurous will subconsciously respond more readily to warm colors than to cool ones. Warm colors advance to the eye and quicken the pulse (also a sign of sexual arousal), while cool colors recede and decelerate the pulse. Hues with a fair measure of red are much warmer, more advancing, than hues heavy with receding blue. Purple—a combination of red and blue—can be a sexual tease; how purple is worn with other hues determines how sexy a color it is. But purple is always intriguing, even mysterious, owing to its internal tension, and mystery, for many, is a part of sexual attraction.

Neutral colors are just that—neutral in their proclamation of sex appeal. A costume of total gray is ambiguous. If the shapes and textures are sexy, so will be gray. But when the shapes and textures are emphatically unsexy, grays (and all other neutrals) are totally sexless.

Black and white are not black-and-white colors. White has its virginal connotations, but it is also a color easily soiled—so it can imply ripening sexuality about to burst, especially when worn with sexy shades. Black is the color of death and evil, but it also has the sinister appeal of forbidden knowledge and worldly sophistication. But black can also conjure up a nun's habit or priestly vestments. No, black and white are not black-and-white colors. As with the other hues, how you wear them ultimately affects your sexual magnetism.

PSYCHOLOGY

As is very evident from the foregoing discussions, individual garments carry their own psychological aspects. Part of the sexual appeal of plain white T-shirts, despite their ubiquity, is the fact that not so long ago they were indeed worn as underwear. That they now appear as the body's outer layer implicitly suggests some sexual availability. Perhaps surprisingly, this effect is compounded when a solid-color T-shirt is worn under a sport coat: it's as if one layer of clothing has already been conveniently removed to facilitate disrobing.

BELOW: Although this outfit doesn't knock you over the head with its sexuality, it is sexy as well as sporty, because the outfit looks "lived in." Perfectly laundered and fastidiously ironed athletic clothes look neither sporty or sexy, only prissy. Here, the dirty knee pads and the worn sneakers prove that the fellow actually indulges in sports and isn't a pretender. Model: Bob Martens.

ABOVE. *Sometimes something as vague as "garment psychology" must be analyzed. This singularly unusual shirt is based on the wing-collar formal style, except that it has an extra band behind the wings, so it's really a cross between a band-collar and a wing-collar shirt. The seamed front has a sewn-in bib.*

Although formality and sexuality are often mutually exclusive, the fact that this intriguing shirt is worn casually with the top button unfastened —to showcase the neck—implies that the wearer is open to experimentation. Shirt: Andrew Fezza. Model: Jim Catch.

RIGHT. *Theoretically, one might assume that unusual underwear would be sexier than the commonplace variety. In practice, however, "honesty" in styling and detailing may be sexier than coy decorative touches or unfunctional gimmicks. Old-fashioned jockey shorts are sexier than would-be sexy novelties. Model: Benjamin Hobbins. Photographed in Venice, Italy.*

Visible zippers always present a temptation to unzip them, to put a hand in and to get nearer the body. This is also true of visible pockets as opposed to ones secreted in a garment with only a barely visible slit for entry.

Asymmetrical closures—say, a shirt that buttons off to one side of the chest—are sexier than centered up-and-down button closures because they're more intriguing, out of the ordinary.

But when the essential integrity of an article of clothing is tampered with, suspicions are aroused. Take something as seemingly simple as male underpants.

While it's true your undershorts are seldom on public display, it's also true that your underwear is almost always the last of your garments your partner sees before coupling gets down to its essence. If you're both in passion's throes, your skivvies shouldn't make or break the event. But the wrong underwear can be a turn-off.

If you think nylon novelty briefs with coy or risqué drawings and mottoes are sexy, think again. Novelty skivvies advertised in the rear pages of slick magazines are just that—novelties, the stuff of jokes. Treating your private parts as a laughing matter is about as unsexy as you can get. Sex can be lighthearted, but only puerile adolescents guffaw at corny sexual innuendo.

See-through underwear that offers a preview of what's later to be unveiled might seem sexy in the abstract, but is seldom so in the reality. Flesh-colored pouches that squeeze you inside them constrict your manhood and distort your physical attributes. See-through underwear just doesn't look "normal," and wearing it could send out a signal that you are abnormally involved with your own pubis. It's okay to like yourself, but not passionately.

Flyless bikini underwear isn't necessarily unsexy, but it doesn't come across as truly authentic or honest. At base, bikini briefs are hypocritical, pretending to be what they're not. They're *not* swimming gear, which a precipitate dip in a pool discloses all too clearly. And they are *not* engineered as true undershorts should be; lacking a fly, bikini briefs imply either that men wearing them never have to urinate or that these men sit down when they take a leak. Striped or patterned bikini briefs appear decorative, not functional.

Some say that boxer shorts are sexy because of their lack of restriction. They can be sexy when that's all you're wearing, but beware: their lack of restriction can be apparent beneath trousers, when more of you than is considered modest is discernible.

The sexiest underwear is plain white underwear, the type commonly referred to as jockey underwear. (Jockey is actually a brand name that has assumed generic connotations.) What is sexy about this utilitarian underclothing? Its directness; its lack of pretension. Jockey underwear is forthrightly masculine.

Needless to say, you may encounter a prospective mate who goes gaga over red flannel long johns; but we're dealing with the laws of probability.

To sum up: when the essential integrity of a garment is tampered with, suspicions are aroused. Another case in point: since a suit is mostly an on-duty outfit, you would never tamper with it so greatly as to transform the trousers into short shorts in a woebegone attempt to make the ensemble sexy.

Now that we've examined the variables of shape, texture, color and/or pattern and garment psychology, let's explore the classifications of male garb to determine which types carry the most sex appeal.

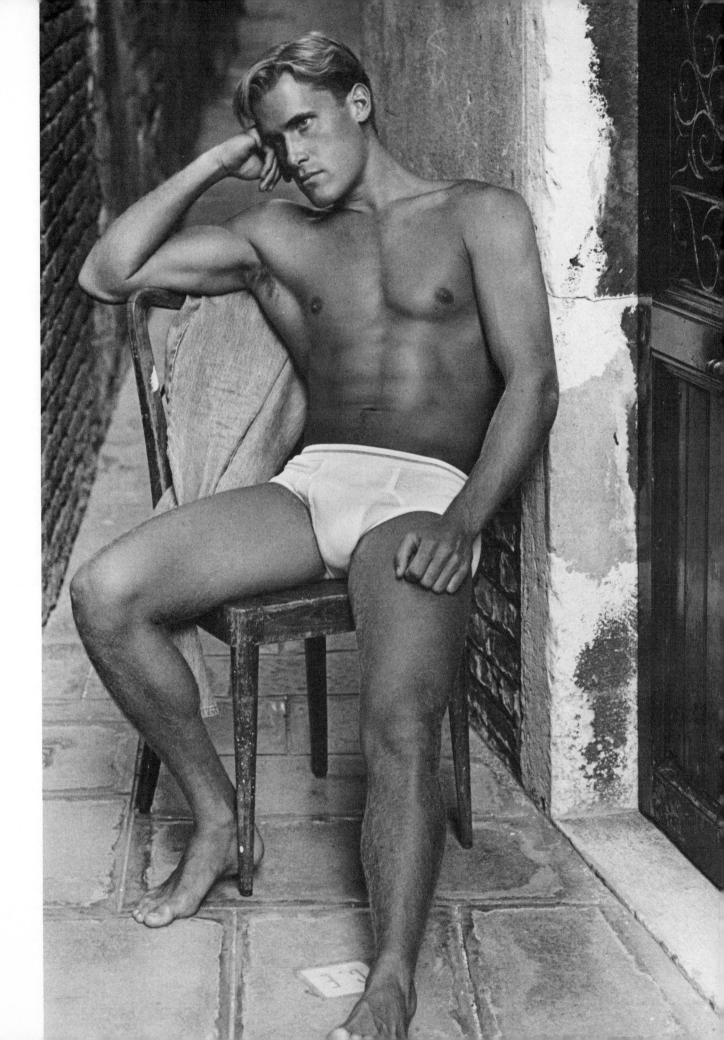

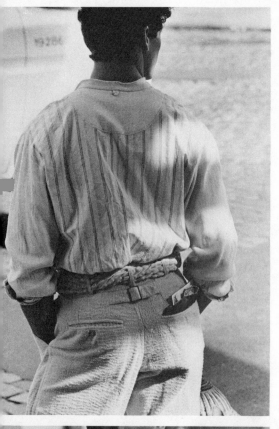

PANTS

As already touched upon, the first requisite for trousers to convey sexiness is that they accentuate the behind. This can be accomplished in several ways. The most obvious is simply to wear tight pants. This ploy is more acceptable in off-duty garb than in dressier varieties. Pants can also be engineered with tucks and seams for a three-dimensional effect to contour the buttocks (in much the same way that women's blouses can be cut to create the impression of full breasts). The fine points of tailoring are impossible to describe, but one way to see how pants accent your backside (or don't) is by looking in a three-way mirror. (That's also a way to determine whether your beam is too broad for you to risk accentuating it. To highlight an unattractive behind isn't sexy; it's mistakenly silly.)

Self-belting pants—ones with extension belts that are built into the waistband and that usually hook or button onto the waistband—almost never project sexiness because they're associated with retirees in senior-citizen communities. Although it's an untrue stereotype, energetic sexuality conjures up visions of youth.

Whatever the waist or fly treatment, the waistline must appear firm, the abdomen flat and the hips as narrow as possible, so love handles must never slide over the waistband and the abdomen can't look convex. For these reasons, pleated pants convey sexiness on a slender, well-built body but not on plump ones.

Sometimes flyless slacks are sexy—particularly if the fabric is lightweight, suggesting pajama bottoms. This is doubly the case when the flyless slacks have drawstring waists . . . and triply so if the drawstring is exposed, psychologically ready to be undone. In general, unconventional fly treatments are sexier than standard ones because subliminally they focus more attention on the crotch without being too flagrant about it. Even low-crotched pants can be sexy, if other elements are also present, because they convey genital freedom. To work, low crotches should accompany roomy thigh proportions (intimating muscled thighs beneath) and tapering legs. Conversely, short-fly treatments are also sexy when accompanying close-to-the-body thigh proportions, explaining the success of timeworn, button-fly-front jeans in certain circles. Such jeans have the extra advantage of clinging softly to the body.

Leather or suede pants are especially sexy if they're not worn as part of a head-to-toe leather or suede ensemble. Knitted pants are seldom sexy because they're too banal, except when they're styled to look like a form of sweat pants. Then the athletic imagery takes over, imparting a ready-for-action appeal.

In certain very casual settings, brightly colored pants are sexy because they imply an adventurous nature. In less free environments, earthy colors are preferred above blues and other cool colors.

SHIRTS

How shirts are styled affects the degree to which they highlight the prized male attributes of a robust neck, broad shoulders, expansive chest and strong biceps.

To accent the neck effectively, sport shirts should be worn with collar open. Band-collar shirts—ones completely lacking collars—do an even better job of presenting the neck openly, but if a neck is stringy, they're counterproductive.

In general, unusual collar treatments help convey sexiness by distinguishing the neck and by subconsciously underscoring the wearer's willingness to experiment, to try out new techniques.

Shoulder treatments—such as epaulets or yokes—help convey the impression of broadened shoulders, so they help impart sexiness.

The chest can appear more expansive via several means. Unbuttoning a shirt to the breastbone calls more obvious attention to the chest . . . and may divulge an underdeveloped one. However, don't forget that familiarity can indeed breed contempt, particularly when sartorial ploys become clichés. Time was when a large number of men tried to proclaim their sexual availability by wearing tight knit shirts unbuttoned nearly to their navels and by bedecking their necks and bared chests with a profusion of gold chains. So familiar did this guise become that it degenerated into cliché. Dressing in this manner today is exceptionally unsexy. Now, if you plan to unbutton a few extra buttons, do so in a fairly roomy woven shirt, signaling that a hand can easily slip inside without a huge effort. That is the real appeal of today's roomier shirts—their openness. Tight shirts appear sexy only on highly developed chests, where the tightness seems to be a natural consequence of the sizable musculature. Old-fashioned ribbed undershirts and tank tops take the easy route by simply exposing more flesh. Mesh shirts do the same. With more subtlety, linen and other natural-fabric open-weave shirts give a hint of flesh without totally revealing it. Often what isn't revealed is sexier than what is, allowing onlookers to complete the stripping in their imaginations. At nudist colonies, ubiquitous flesh quickly loses all its eroticism.

Naturally, stripes and patterns encircling the chest also subliminally draw more emphasis to it and visually expand it.

So-called muscle shirts, with their sharply abbreviated sleeve length, are a quick way to point out strong biceps. Rolling up sleeves above the biceps is another.

Dress shirts—ones designed specifically to be worn with ties and suits—aren't sexy by their very nature, since they tend to look earnest.

Tactile weaves and knits are sexier than hard, flat surfaces. Shirts in warm, advancing colors are sexier than those in neutral or receding hues.

SWEATERS

Because sweaters are styled in so many ways, they can project many different traits, sometimes more than one simultaneously. When they're worn to convey a mixture of characteristics, the strength of any one expression is diluted, but other garments can be enlisted to sharpen the focus. Although seldom purely sexy, the right sweater can contribute to an outfit's sex appeal.

Turtleneck sweaters are essentially lacking in sexiness because they cover up the neck, implying that the neck is vulnerable, not robust. Strongly identified with the "beat generation" and "eggheads" of any decade, dark turtlenecks also carry the imagery of intellectualism, which—rightly or wrongly—isn't usually thought of as sexy.

Most cardigans, with their grandfatherly or professorial connotations, are likewise essentially unsexy, primarily because they usually conceal the buttocks beneath their shapelessness. One exception is the varsity cardigan on campus: this sweater is an icon for athletic prowess, so it has associations extraneous to the garment itself. However, when worn by males obviously past their college years, varsity sweaters are rather pathetic, suggesting that the wearer is hung up on past glory days and has little prospect for an equally glorious future. Sports-derived sweaters—ones whose stylistic origins are intimately connected with sporting activities without being the actual gear (such as "tennis" sweaters that never see the court)—have a visual vitality that can be interpreted as being sexy . . . but more likely will be perceived as simply being sporty. However, since athleticism and sexiness are strongly linked, a sweater that smacks of sportiness may convey a secondary impression of sexiness.

ABOVE. The burliness of this sweater adds optical dimension to the torso, while the horizontal movement of the pattern makes both the chest and the biceps appear stronger—emphatically so, since the man has strong muscular definition to begin with.

The scarf is wrapped neatly, so as to seem almost integral to the sweater; this creates an extra element of interest around his robust neck.

That the sweater and scarf—both deeply textural—are in warm, advancing hues adds to the sensuality of the outfit. Sweater & scarf: G. Maislinger. Model: Bryan Coolahan.

RIGHT. Possessing a sexy body is a great asset in projecting sexiness, particularly when glimpses of that body are presented with an implicit tease.

The hot orange, sexily hued mesh shirt totally—and deliberately—fails to cover this fellow's very tight tank top, which reveals almost as much of his torso as if it were bare.

The military-type belt carries sexual imagery, and the faded jeans are far from roomy. Sunglasses: Ray-Ban. Model: Richard Villella.

LEFT. *Even at a distance, the high visibility of primary red is a primary reason the color is sexy: it captures attention and excites the pulse. Hence the sexiness of this bright red jacket, which incidentally is constructed to build out the shoulders to make it sexy in shape as well as color.*

Although smooth textures aren't inherently sexy, these trousers have an unexpected luster to stimulate eye appeal, and the unusual striping also arouses interest.

The tactile knit shirt has an atypical no-collar neckline, plus an inset of contrasting fabric for the buttons, to frame the man's neck, likewise contributing to the outfit's sexiness. Clothing: Roger Forsythe. Model: David Spiewak. Photographed on the Brooklyn Bridge.

BELOW. *More sexy red, this time in a jacket with a fleece lining in two colors to add spark as well as sensual tactility. The bold geometry of the brightly colored sweater draws onlookers' eyes to the man's chest, one of the highly rated parts of the physique. Jacket: Charivari 72. Model: Lou LaRusso.*

RIGHT. *Sexy red again, on sweat shorts that tell the world this is a "tuf" customer. Juxtaposed with the athletic shorts is a luxurious silk robe in strong, vibrant colors that cause heads to turn.*

To be honest, this European and Australian heavyweight karate champion's body doesn't require much external assistance to gain notice. Robe: Fernando Sanchez. Model: Hans Lundgren.

LEFT. *Buttons and buttons, zippers and zippers, metal studs and snaps —the profusion of ways to "enter" this outfit (with the shirt already well opened to facilitate visual entry to the chest through the mesh T-shirt) tantalizes in a way that more conventionally detailed garments do not. But this outfit has other sexy details as well.*

The military-in-origin epaulets extend the shoulder line, while the bomber style of the jacket—likewise from a military background—stops at the waist to allow rear view of the rear and front view of the exposed buttons on the fly to play up the crotch without being crude about it.

Another military touch is the belt, and military styling almost always has an aura of sexuality. Model: Benjamin Hobbins.

BELOW. *And fur is also almost always sensual. This rich fur-lined jacket certainly is.*

Belonging to the red color family, the claret ground of this sweater has only slightly less passionate appeal than primary red, and the horizontal geometric pattern optically enlarges the chest while the hand-loomed scarf caresses the neck with innuendo. Jacket: Cleo & Pat. Sweater: Gianfranco Ruffini. Pants: Daniel Caron. Scarf: Susan Horton. Model: Tony Stephano.

By virtue of its design, the sexiest sweater is a V-neck style, because the V of the neckline implies the favored V-shaped physique. When worn with an open-neck shirt, a V-neck sweater also highlights the neck. Detailing along the V—such as geometric patterning—is another reinforcement.

Whereas the style of a sweater affects its sexiness, color and texture are truly more important than mere shape. Per usual, tactile textures and rich or offbeat colors are the sexiest.

SUITS

Even when they're worn for purposes other than business, suits send out fundamentally on-duty signals. Seldom is a suit worn for fun. However, suits are sometimes worn for social occasions, so technically they are sometimes off-duty garb. But can a suit be sexy? When you hear a woman rhapsodizing about how sexy men look in suits, be convinced she's thinking less about the bed than of hearth and home: smartly tailored suits usually convey a sense of social, behavioral and economic stability—good attributes in a husband, though these characteristics may have nothing to do with sexual expertise.

Not many suits are sexy, not even on men with terrific builds, because most American suits "tent" the body instead of accentuating it. This is particularly true of suits in the so-called Ivy (or Preppy or natural-shoulder) style—that style most associated with businessmen in the Brooks Brothers mold. Engineered shape, such as the suggestion of a waistline, is taboo in this school of dress. Similarly, the suit trousers are straight-legged from the hip to the (uncuffed) cuff, and the fly is relatively deep, the rear relatively roomy, thereby deemphasizing any anatomical parts. As a result, a man inside an Ivy (or Preppy or natural-shoulder) suit tends to assume H-shape proportions—undesirable proportions when it comes to transmitting sexual magnetism, although the same proportions are considered desirable in certain business settings.

Suits in a more British vein don't always have lightly padded shoulders (although they often do), but the suit coats are almost always fitted closer to the body, with a suggestion of shape at the waist and with a little flare around the hips. The suit pants also tend to adhere more closely to the physique in that they are less full at the knee than at the thigh. Overall, the outline of the British-type suit is tapering, imparting V-shaped proportions.

Suits in the European mode (even if they're manufactured in America or Hong Kong) have even more shape to them than British-styled suits. These more body-conforming suit coats and pants suggest Y-shaped proportions.

It's probably true that you'll look less "businessy" in a British or European suit than in that professional paragon, the American Ivy suit. And you will definitely look less sexy in an Ivy suit than in prototypical British or European models.

"High-fashion" suits—those more experimental in shape—are occasionally introduced. Their impression is harder to predict. For some viewers, the novelty of the avant-garde translates into sexual appeal. For others, novelty can be perceived as eccentric. High-fashion clothing always commands attention, which may not always be positive. Generally, however, if avant-garde suits don't deviate too far from the desirable V- and Y-shapes, they have a very good chance of appearing more sexy than traditionally styled suits.

Of course, a suit's outlined shape isn't all that contributes to or detracts from its sexiness. Naturally, a very significant factor is fabric.

Serge, a fabric often used in moderately priced suits, isn't particu-

BELOW. Suits are seldom expressly sexy because they are strongly associated with on-duty garb—clothing that's often worn out of a sense of obligation or enforced propriety rather than personal choice. Avant-garde suits, however, can impart some sexiness because they may indicate an adventurous spirit that won't be whipped into convention.

Suit and sport jackets with widened shoulders and waist suppression are more body-conscious than "sack" suits. The position of the notch formed by the meeting of coat collar and lapel also affects sexiness. Here the notch is relatively low, accompanied by a relatively low button closure on the body of the jacket, to elongate the V shape, thereby magnifying its sexual magnetism.

The kinetic energy of the intricate check pattern is more intriguing than a solid color or a more customary controlled plaid. The napped surface of the flannel slacks has greater tactility—and sexual appeal—than a harder fabric.

In huge generalization, sport-coat combinations tend to be sexier than suits because they are less formally reserved. Jacket & tie: Charivari 72. Model: Lou LaRusso.

larly sensual to the eye or to the touch because it is durably smooth-surfaced, without a visible hint of luxury or softness. Flannel, on the other hand, looks—and is—softer to the touch because the surface is lightly brushed to create a nap. Because of their nubbiness, tweeds are likewise more sensual than smooth-surfaced fabrics. Smooth surfaces suggest coolness; tactile fabrics imply body warmth.

Color can't be overlooked. One of the most popular suit colors is navy blue. Navy blue is also an unsexy color. The color blue conveys a subconscious sense of reserve and restraint—attributes that have no place in sexual encounters. Navy blue—among the densest shades of blue—is reserved and restrained in the extreme.

As you know, the color red epitomizes passion; but Saint Nick is the only guy who can carry off a red suit. Brown is an earthy hue. Since good sex is earthy, brown is a lustier shade than blue. But very dark brown approaches black, the sinister color of death (and morticians). Mid-toned or pale brown is more "affectionate" than dark brown, because white added to any color dispels heavy-toned severity. A slightly pinkish cast to a mid-toned brown adds a subtle (and subliminal) hint of red, making the hue a little sexier. But, as is always the case, what really counts is the total package.

Patterns in suits are generally neutral, neither sexy nor unsexy. Stripes or plaids or solids are questions of personal taste.

(A more detailed exploration of the suiting world is found in Part II: On-Duty Garb.)

SHORTS

Back to a clothing category definitely in the off-duty mode.

Walking shorts (as distinguished from underwear or gym shorts) reveal the calves, and sometimes some of the thighs, but this exposure doesn't automatically make shorts sexy apparel. Toddlers invariably wear shorts, so shorts can sometimes suggest infantilism. Happily, the world doesn't abound in pedophiles, so babyish shorts with integral suspenderlike straps to keep the shorts from falling are seldom considered sexy.

Because most adult males cover their legs in most situations, except at beaches or resorts, even partially bared legs always cause a greater visual stir than trousered ones. Learned associations determine how attention-getting walking shorts are read by onlookers.

Bermuda shorts, which reach nearly to the kneecaps in a stovepipe fashion and which have very little extraneous detailing, are principally associated with the 1950s. They have fairly conservative connotations and hence are not strong on sex appeal.

By contrast, jams—usually of a lightweight material, with a drawstring waist—are more steeped in the surfing mystique, evoking freedom and adventure and sexuality.

Khaki and safari shorts suggest rugged sexuality, particularly when they are detailed with buckled straps and zippers and pockets with a hint of the military about them.

Athletics-derived shorts enjoy the sensual linkage that always accompanies clothing associated with physical activity.

Cut-offs—formerly long pants or jeans transformed into shorts by scissor action—give the impression of total disregard for clothing to the point of destroying a garment in order to free the body from constraint. Some may find this sexy; others may find this violent or scary.

"Hot pants," very tight, tiny and revealing, are too bonded to female pinups to pass as sexy on males.

Recently, voluminous-legged, baggy shorts—the antithesis of what

RIGHT. Some garments are imbued with "feelings" because of ingrained connotations. Shorts reminiscent of jams project sexiness because of their association with the surfing scene. Because surfers seem to embody freedom, adventure and sexuality, jams gain in sexiness because of this evocation.

Here, the exposed drawstring is another successful ploy to inject greater subliminal sexiness. Model: Russell Henis.

is usually thought of as sexy—have been taken up by a number of young males. These styles, usually pleated, are often worn with chest- and/or biceps-revealing casual shirts, but sometimes with purposefully oversized sweaters or sweat shirts. The sexiness of the shorts probably stems from reverse psychology, calling more subconscious attention to male privates by withdrawing them absolutely from view: what could possibly be lurking inside the folds of those shorts that requires so much extravagant room to hide?

SWIM TRUNKS

In some secluded corners, the most popular bathing attire is a bare behind. In general, however, swimwear that's too revealing is deemed revolting, particularly at public parks. So much as a glimpse of pubic hair is a critical no-no. Beware bikinis.

As with underwear, where basic briefs are the sexiest because they are functional, uncluttered by negative associations, bathing briefs are sexier than too revealing, flagrant styles. Although most briefs are flyless, some have nonfunctional fly details. By subtly calling attention to the crotch without being obvious or intimidating about it, these are slightly sexier than the more conventional flyless brief.

As with purposefully voluminous walking shorts, sometimes baggy boxer trunks convey sexiness if they're colored or patterned in a funky, offbeat way. But drab boxer trunks are more likely to imply that their wearer is a nerd.

Truthfully, when all is said and done, because so much of the body is exposed in swimwear, the sexiest trunks, whatever their basic style, are whichever ones adorn very good bodies, provided they don't overexpose.

LEFT. Taking clothing out of its usual setting can give it more appeal than when it's discovered in a more orthodox context . . . or it can be overly jarring.

Here the terry-cloth robe seems logical and functional, since you can sense the proximity of a swimming pool without seeing it. That's why the effect is one of sexiness, not inconsistency. Robe: George Graham Galleries. Model: Jim Catch.

RIGHT. Swim briefs do a hell of a job of revealing flesh. If the physique revealed isn't up to snuff, no swimwear can manufacture sexiness. But very skimpy bikinis are too flagrant to be sexy even on splendid bodies.

Swim costumes that overexpose most often have more turn-off than turn-on appeal . . . except for people who are heavily into skin. Swimwear: Laguna. Models (left to right): Steve Finehirsh, Richard Villella, Gregory Osgan.

SLEEPWEAR

Sleepwear exists as much to be seen in as to sleep in. Coy or cutesy nightshirts are not sexy. Pajamas made of material that feels sensual next to your skin look sensual to another's eyes and feel sensual to another's touch.

Robes aren't worn to bed, but they're mentally linked to sleepwear. When worn outside the bedtime context, sleepwear assumes a stronger aura of sexuality—or comedy—than when the garments are put to their intended use. One reason onlookers find a luxurious terry-cloth robe sexy at poolside goes way beyond its function to dry the body and keep chills under control: the robe's nocturnal role is juxtaposed with the public display of flesh, and the imagination (without consciously even making the connection) leaps. Pants that are obviously slacks but styled with some pajama-bottom imagery are also sexy because they bring bedroom activity subconsciously to mind. However, honest-to-goodness pajama bottoms worn on the street would be comedic because they would be so incongruous. Similarly, pajama tops would never pass muster as sport shirts; they too would look comedic. But out-and-out sport shirts styled with pajama collars gain sexuality from the subliminal bedroom connection.

FOOTWEAR

Although the first requisite of shoes is to coordinate with an outfit, footwear, like all clothing articles, can project sensuality—or other attributes. Shoes don't necessarily do so overtly; it's a matter of nuance. And the nuances shift according to the outfit under investigation.

ABOVE. These pajamas are sexy because a well-muscled man is wearing them; they would not be nearly as sexy on a less attractive physique. But a less than perfectly built male will still look sexier in these pajamas than in woolly flannels.

While soft fabrics are sexy in clothing worn in public, smooth materials, especially lustrous ones, make the sexiest sleepwear because of hedonistic connotations.

Since stripes are strongly associated with maleness, striped pajamas also rate high in the sexy department. Model: Matthew J. Williams.

Except for foot fetishists, exposed toes are not thrilling. In fact, rubber thongs worn with long pants are antisexual: they arouse images of celibate religious leaders tending their flocks. Worn with shorts or beachwear, rubber thongs are sexually neutral, seemingly worn for convenience and no other reason. The same can be said of sandals, although their styling is greatly more varied than thongs. Dress sandals may be chic or sophisticated, but hardly ever sexy in their own right. And beware of wearing strongly patterned socks with childish-looking sandals.

Most lace-up shoes are dressier than slip-ons. Since dressier means more formal, and since formality and sexuality are almost mutually exclusive, most lace-up shoes fail to project any sexual magnetism. However, suede or grained-leather lace-ups have more tactility than smooth leathers and consequently are less unsexy than smooth-leathered lace-ups. The dressiest shoe around is the formal patent leather pump, which also happens to be a slip-on. It is an exception to the rule that slip-ons are by nature sexier than lace-ups.

Slip-ons are sexy (to the extent that shoes ever are truly sexy) because they also slip off: clothing that's easily removed without effort and fuss tends to convey freer sexuality than clothing difficult to get out of.

Because they don't slip on and off with ease, boots are not inherently sexy. However, some boots are rich in imagery that adds to their sexiness. Heeled boots also alter the body's center of gravity, elongating the leg (and by implication the penis) while also making the chest and buttocks more prominent; thus, heeled boots alter the apparent sexiness of the body itself. Cowboy lore boosts the sex

RIGHT. *Footwear is not the sexiest clothing category, but even boots project small nuances that add to an outfit's total impression. Heeled boots alter the body's center of gravity, causing the chest to thrust forward and the behind to firm up and out, thereby emphasizing two prime male attributes. The higher the heel, the more noticeable the effect. In this case, since the heels are only slightly elevated, the boots will affect the man's stance minimally. In cowboy boots with extreme heel elevation, however, the change can be very dramatic. Boots: Fratelli. Model: Cris Byars.*

appeal of cowboy boots, although wearing cowboy boots may suggest you're a fraud if you're unfamiliar with the range. In some circles, construction boots are considered sexy, but they can also contain elements of overly purposeful costuming. Boots are difficult to assess in the abstract. Even more than shoes, they must be viewed outfit by outfit.

Socks seldom make huge individual statements either. Plain, dark dress socks always lack whammy when conventionally worn. Bright red athletic socks that have pizzazz when paired with gym shorts lack credibility when worn by a priest. Generally, however, when it comes to off-duty garb, atypical sock styles—such as Argyles in pastel shades—generate more visual interest, which is commensurate with generating more sex appeal, than standard dress hosiery. Even so, socks that scream to be seen throw an outfit off balance; what's the gain in shifting your visual focus to your ankles?

OUTERWEAR

As the term implies, outerwear is worn out of doors as the outer layer of clothing, and is different from clothing that is worn indoors . . . usually. A sweater coat, for instance, is little else than an overgrown cardigan sweater that can be worn for protection from the elements but that might also be worn indoors, particularly if a landlord is skimpy with the heat.

Since outerwear exists more for practicality than for fashionability, it doesn't send out very strong attitudinal symbols. Still, if you peer very closely, you'll discern some.

Dress coats are worn primarily to make a man look proper in structured dress settings. Their very correctness interferes with projecting sexiness. But some dress coats have fur collars, and fur is a touchteaser; fur surrounding the excitable neck area can seem to indicate the wearer's sensual nature. Wrap coats—ones that overlap in front, generally with no visible buttons but secured by a belt that usually ties but may buckle—suggests that the body beneath likes to be hugged, since the effect of a wrap coat is very similar to an embrace.

Trench coats, though originally embellished with yokes, shoulder flaps and multitudinous pockets, are now often simply serviceable, nondescript outerwear, a type worn by both men and women with very little sexual stylistic distinction. As such, the unembellished trench coat is unsexily androgynous. Even its symbolism for errant flashers helps undermine the trench coat's sex appeal. On the other hand, when styled with authentic (more or less) military details, the trench coat becomes more swashbuckling. In fact, military inspirations add swagger to outerwear in general. Bomber jackets have manly, warfaring origins and also the decided advantage of extending no farther than the waist, allowing hip visibility. Most Space Age jackets are also waist-hugging items with a romantic past and future.

Shearling-lined coats, whether short or long in length, appear at once rugged and sensual.

FORMALWEAR

It's difficult to think of formalwear—dinner jackets and the like—as off-duty garb, but there are times a man willingly, even smilingly, dons a black tie . . . or apricot tails.

To be blunt, apricot tails are not sexy; they're silly, the saccharine confection of formalwear rental specialists catering to youthful romanticism—and undeveloped taste.

But classic dinner jackets aren't sexy either, because they ensure

RIGHT. Outerwear is generally more concerned with being utilitarian than with enhancing the wearer's attributes. But more than utility can be conveyed in distinctive outerwear.

Shearling-lined coats capitalize on the masculine-laden lore of the West. On top of this charged sexual imagery, shearling coats also convey sensuality by encasing the neck and framing the face with a deep, lush texture. This particular glove-leather shearling coat is highly sensual in its own right; but the sexiness of the outfit doesn't stop there.

The neck of the sweater is unconventionally square and revealing when worn without a shirt beneath. The pants are leather, but textured with small stripes to control any overly leathered decadence. And the pants are snug in the butt and hips. The military belt isn't menacing but whimsical. Still, military imagery evokes sex.

Strong sensuality is conveyed without crossing the line of tastelessness. Outfit: Andrew Fezza. Model: Todd Bentley.

that men recede, each looking uniformly like the others in basic guise. Liberties must be taken with the classic formalwear looks if any sexiness is to be imparted. A bright red satin bow tie, for example, can supplant the traditional black one. Cummerbunds customarily match the color and fabric of the bow tie.

But other liberties can be taken too, depending upon how adventurous you are and if you remember the guideline that more formal events generally have more stringent dress expectations. Some designers are now offering alternatives to the standard dinner jacket. When these alternatives are extremely body-conscious (as some of them are), they're sexy as well as adventurous. When they're not especially body-conscious, they can look adventurous, if not explicitly sexy. When sizing up formalwear alternatives, always remember the truths of the V-, Y- and T-shaped proportions.

ACCESSORIES

Accessories are those articles which flesh out an outfit but which, strictly speaking, are unnecessary. Take belts. Most pants won't drop off without them, so belts aren't really essential. But they do help make an outfit more whole, more complete. Jewelry is an accessory, though hardly a necessity. Occasionally a necessity, neckties are also accessories. Scarves, pocket squares, hats, watches, executive cases

ABOVE. Conventional formalwear—the penguin sort of look—lacks sexiness because it homogenizes. Untraditional "tuxedo" outfits, by contrast, are much more demanding of individual attention.

In this example, the formalwear is sexy as well as attention-getting because it is extremely body-conscious. The to-the-waist-only jacket, called the Spencer style, doesn't obstruct below-the-waist display, while the satin lapels direct attention to the male chest. The shoulders are slightly padded to square off the top.

The wide-in-the-thighs tapering trousers reinforce the sexy V shape.

In a textural weave interspersed with metallic threads, this outfit might be too liberated for stodgy settings. Since formal occasions are often imbued with stringent expectations, you may need guts and the courage of your convictions to flout the D.A.R. Outfit (except tie): Jhane Barnes. Tie: Vicky Davis. Model (also right): Tim Clement.

RIGHT. Accessories are outfit components that supposedly complete the ensemble down to the last— and occasionally superfluous—detail. Sometimes accessories can interfere with an outfit's ability to project a desired characteristic because they clutter up the viewer's line of vision by drawing too much attention to themselves.

A gold chain would have detracted from the sexiness of this sweater because the sensual appeal of the exposed, strong neck would have been undercut. Sweater: G. Maislinger.

and umbrellas are also accessories. Some accessories—wallets, for instance—are seldom even seen.

Most often the fewer accessories worn, the greater the sex appeal. At base, most accessories are decorative, and decorating the body is less sensual than giving the anatomy visual breathing space. Also, most accessories are not designed with sex appeal in mind. A watch can be described as elegant or sturdy but rarely sexy. And while a gold neck chain may draw some attention to a robust neck, it does so somewhat at the expense of the neck per se: an onlooker's eye may—and probably will—be drawn to the neck chain, mentally stopping there and only secondarily registering the neck itself. So, to project optimum sex appeal, keep most accessories to a minimum. For those accessories which remain, make them very intriguing.

PUBLIC UTILITY

Love may or may not be just around the corner, but every time you stroll out your front door you could encounter persons unknown who might become your sexual partners (presumably one at a time). That's why your public appearances should be made only after you've given some consideration to your appearance. As long as you're

RIGHT. Just as sex need not be overly serious, sexy clothing can also be lighthearted, display a sense of humor.

This highly styled outfit could be worn in numerous public situations, from dining to theatergoing to dancing. It combines a sure feeling for forward fashion with subtle sexiness.

Dropped shoulders extend dimensions here. The narrow panel inset carries the sexiness of leather without overdoing it. Stopping at the waist, the jacket leaves an unobstructed view of the unusually deep and full pleated front of the trousers (and of the man's behind should he turn around); its roominess and the tapered line of the trousers make a strong V configuration.

The tab of fabric on the shirt that serves as a very unconventional tie clasp is enough to get conversation going with strangers. Outfit: Matsuda. Model: Jhamil.

dressed, your clothing contributes to the impressions you make. So does personal grooming, even when you're undressed.

When you're going to an expensive restaurant, you shave, right? You should also shave before jaunting to the shoe-repair shop. After all, while waiting your turn at the counter, you might start chatting with an attractive customer in the queue. Later on, if the attraction is mutual, you might want to take that new acquaintance on a date to an expensive restaurant.

Got the message? Always dress for the unexpected but the hoped-for, since hoped-for though unexpected pleasures can materialize.

Naturally, in your quest for new relationships, you won't dress as if for a date at an expensive restaurant if you're only heading for the shoe-repair. As always, you'll dress to the circumstances.

But circumstances shift. Remember that what is appropriately sexy attire in one set of circumstances isn't so in another.

FOOD FOR THOUGHT

Generally, whenever people gather where food is to be served, greater conviviality enters the atmosphere. Imagine a cocktail party without hors d'oeuvres. Probably only true extroverts are nodding to strangers. Now imagine the same party when hors d'oeuvres are being circulated. As strangers lift a canapé from a passing tray, they smile amiably at each other.

The lesson? Since people are more relaxed around food, they are also usually less harshly judgmental. In food-consuming situations, you are allowed more liberty to be expressive in your dress, provided you don't break the unwritten rules about overall crowd expectation. When people are relaxed, they are also more receptive. If projecting sex appeal is your main objective at a dinner party—which it well may not be—the presence of food means you can dress more sexily than if you were attending a library lecture series.

CLOSE ENCOUNTERS

What's on your agenda? Are you attending a small gathering or a mob scene? The smaller the number of people populating a setting, the more likely is it that the individuals will unconsciously seek a cohesive group identity. Clothing is an easily accessible visible bond. Thus, if you dress very sexily at a small gathering and others are not so bedecked, you may be ostracized. Usually, when among limited numbers, it's wiser to soft-pedal an exaggerated trait until personal contact has been established. On the other hand, if you're actively on the make and you manage to attract the right person in that little crowd, hats off to you.

Larger crowds don't place as large a value on homogeneity . . . unless the crowd is composed of Ku Klux Klan members, who are unsexy enough to think that sheets are to be worn instead of romped on. Not only is it difficult to establish an overriding group identity in a large crowd, it's also very hard to stand out in one. That means you can be slightly more overt in projecting a desired attribute, as long as you don't trespass too far beyond the crowd's collective sensibility, such as by wearing hot pants to a diplomatic reception. On the other hand, even at an embassy function, you can insert a hot red silk handkerchief in the breast pocket of your dinner jacket.

ABOVE. Like the outfit on the opposite page, here is an ensemble that's sexy but not in a knock-'em-down manner. The extreme tactility of the sweater is a touch-teaser. Its combination with the tapered slacks creates a V configuration. Outfit: Charivari Workshop. Model: Neil Kramer.

RIGHT. Here is another V-shaped outfit. (The variations are many, since there are many ways to look sexy.)

Not truly epaulets, the fabric panels at the shoulders build up those proportions, while rolling and pushing up the jacket's sleeves fills out the biceps area. The absence of a collar makes the neck more prominent, as does the round-necked sweater.

The linen pants, short in the fly (and, not visible, contoured to the behind) but wide in the thigh, are supposed to wrinkle to look "lived in" . . . which can also translate as "slept in."

Look carefully at the belt: it wraps around twice, not at the waist but at abdomen level, for a lowering of focus—subliminally a sexually charged ploy.

Sexy but not overwhelming, this outfit affords easy entry into a variety of places without risk of censure, yet it sends out subtle erotic signals. In many ways, such subconscious signals are the strongest because they meet less conscious resistance. Outfit: Roger Forsythe.

TERRITORIAL IMPERATIVE

People tend to be protective about their own turf, so when you're invited to someone's home, you are given privileged entry. This act of faith is sometimes accompanied by unease on the part of the inviter: will the sanctity of territory be violated by your entry? Initially at least, you may be on probation. Too strong a projection of sexuality can literally be interpreted as invasive, as you storm the territory with your lusty being. Unless you are very certain that sex is way up there in both your minds, it's not good strategy to come on too strong the first time you set foot in someone's home. Ironically, public places somewhat diffuse an aura of sexuality because the sexually magnetic emanations are transmitted randomly and can be perceived by innocent passersby who aren't purposefully meant to catch the signals. Sexual projection is thus less threatening because it's not potently one-to-one.

On your own turf, projecting stronger sexual signals is more permissible, since a first-time visitor to your pad can finesse an exit if what you think is a knock-'em-dead outfit is seen as a prelude to a knock-'em-down assault. Extremely overpowering sexual imagery is risky in any at-home situation, but less so when the territory is your own. Still, it's wiser to save that knock-'em-dead outfit for a more appropriate place, such as a disco, where you can pull out all the stops.

BELOW. "At-home" garb requires special handling, since dressing in extremely sexy clothing while entertaining (or being entertained) can cause defenses to shoot up instead of lower. Wearing a familiar garment that's "safe"—such as a pair of sweat pants—can lessen the tension that might arise if you appeared in a totally, overtly sexy getup.

But sexiness need not necessarily be greatly reduced . . . if you choose the right, purportedly "safe" garment. For example, these sweat pants are not as innocent as at first they might appear. Pale-colored, they advance more than dark ones do, and the tactility of the velour suggests that touching is definitely no no-no.

With the striped T-shirt placed beneath the overshirt (unbuttoned to the limit), the flesh and sinew of the chest aren't truly exposed, but onlookers are subconsciously more aware that this fellow has a chest worth viewing than if the overshirt were buttoned to the neck. Model: Russel Aron.

INTIMATE KNOWLEDGE

ABOVE. Here's another top that would be extremely chest-revealing —even more so than the one on the opposite page—if it weren't layered with another shirt beneath it. (Actually, this fellow is pulling the tank top down to bare more skin than its already dipping neckline permits without a strategic tug. This ploy works only in warm surroundings; in a cool room, the gesture does not look unrehearsed.)

Because he wears the tank top, the plunging V of the sweater doesn't expose unacceptable amounts of flesh. But it does give an unobstructed view of the tank top, which happens to hug the chest. Not content to stop there, the sweater combines several tactile textures, plus yarns of many warm shades, causing the torso to appear larger—and, you guessed it, sexier.

Strong in sensuality, this is a courting outfit. Perfect for public gatherings, it might come on too strong on private turf. Sweater: G. Maislinger. Tank top: Float. Pants: Hector Herrera. Model: Bryan Coolahan.

Acquaintances react to you differently from the way strangers do. Your voice, your manners, the ideas you express—these and many additional clues to your unique personal identity color others' reactions once the formalities of introductions are over. Sexy clothing *can* help you attract prospective mates. Sexy clothing *may* handicap you in meeting other prospective mates who fear the intimacy that sexual attraction leads to. With certain prospective mates, you might make greater headway by projecting friendliness (or sophistication or sportiness) rather than sexuality. If you come on like gangbusters, you may be unknowingly screening out strangers who are repelled by gangbuster tactics. Think about it. But if you're too sexually timid in your clothing, you might miss a hell of a time.

After you've attracted a prospective mate, you will probably choose to highlight some aspect of your sensuality to some degree. After all, that's what we've been exploring throughout this entire chapter—the question of how much, if any, sexiness to convey under specific circumstances. Once intimacy is established, *projecting* sensuality is no longer a compelling need: now the ebb-and-flow of human intercourse—not merely imagistic signals or symbols—takes over. At this stage, you dress for your mate's and your own enjoyment . . . and occasionally still to the expectations of the outside world. With romance fulfilled, you can turn to weighing how clothing can be utilized to achieve other varieties of personal fulfillment. In fact, even if you haven't yet attracted your ideal partner, you probably won't want to spend every waking hour dressing to be sexy. The sad facts are, we can't spend our entire lives in bed—and, believe it or not, there's more to life than getting our jollies.

CHAPTER 2
CRISP!

MR. CLEAN

Now that you know how to turn yourself into a paragon of sensuality, recognize that if you wear only extremely sexy outfits day after day, night after night, people may suspect that your libido needs leashing. Dressing the free way allows you to show off different aspects of your personality by dressing differently for different moods and occasions. And not all moods and occasions are laden with sex.

For many of life's dealings, you will come out ahead if you project an image of upbeat decorum. (Pay particular attention to that adjective "upbeat," which we'll define momentarily.) In general, a decorous individual is mindful of social conventions and purposefully says or does nothing that could seem rude or boorish. Such a person *conforms* to the code of socially acceptable behavior, to the laws of etiquette. In clothing matters, a decorous person toes the line and never offends.

But herdlike conformity in all matters—clothing and otherwise—isn't a positive virtue, and blandness isn't necessarily attractive. Nice is nice, but too nice is boring.

An upbeat person knows all the rules of the game but doesn't shrink from bending some of them when those rules are outmoded or nonsensical. Thus, an upbeat person knows the *real* score, is no naif, no blind follower.

Upbeat decorum encompasses the "knowingness" and the personal integrity, also bravery, to cut through stodgy and meaningless convention to come up with an individual code without trampling the rights or sensibilities of others.

Upbeat decorum is a phrase that can also be applied to a style of dress—a style that retains elements of the conventional without being predictable. A one-word description of this style is Crisp!

LEFT. Clothing in the crisp style is never startling, but it isn't totally familiar either. Take these shorts. They come in a conventional length that's not too short or too long; at first glance, they don't bowl you over. But a second glance reveals the unusual buckle detailing at each side of the waistband. Though related to Bermuda shorts, these take an extra stylistic step, earning them the Crisp label.

On the other hand, appearing shirtless interferes with projecting crispness, since the crisp mode isn't noted for its physicality. Shorts: Alan Flusser. Model: Cameron Hall.

DATE BOOK

When you dress in a crisp manner, you're constantly performing a juggling act with your clothing, tossing tradition, innovation and moderation into the atmosphere in new combinations.

First, tradition. Some pieces of clothing have traditional connotations and traditionally are accepted by large numbers of people as being "correct" garb. Oxford-cloth button-down-collared shirts fit into this category. So do knit polo shirts, chino trousers and Bermuda shorts.

Next, innovation. Travel to any middle-class suburb in the United States and you're sure to discover several men wearing pale blue button-down shirts and tan chinos. Odds are also high that you'll come across several other men in red polo shirts and navy/gray/pale blue plaid Bermuda shorts. That is not innovation.

During your suburban trip, you *might* catch sight of *one* man wearing a peach button-down shirt striped with shades of jade and ruby, paired with dove gray chinos. Or *one* man wearing a turquoise polo shirt with a magenta collar trimmed with neon yellow, combined with Bermuda shorts in a rainbow of gem hues. That is innovation.

Now, moderation. If you happened upon the guy wearing the dove gray chinos with the peach shirt striped with jade and ruby, you witnessed the crisp style in action. The basic style of the shirt and pants is traditional, while the colors are innovative, but only moderately so, in no way shocking.

What about the fellow in the gem-hued plaid Bermudas and the vivid polo shirt? His style is not crisp. The colors are just a little too daring—too immoderate—for that description. But the colors are exciting, even tasteful, if not restful. The outfit works very well . . . in an entirely different style, one called Smart! (You'll check out that adventurous style in Chapter 7.)

Let's recolor this outfit more moderately. The shirt would be fine if the shorts were a solid tan, thereby taming the shirt's aggressive colors. Similarly, a basic white (or almost any pastel-colored) polo shirt would temper the fieriness of the shorts, making the sum of the parts moderate.

Here's a general guideline for the crisp mode of dressing: If the cut of the garments is fairly traditional—and it should be—when the colors of the individual garments are only moderately innovative, the overall effect of the outfit will be crisply moderate. However, if any one garment is strongly innovative in style or color, then a more traditional garment is required to strike a moderate balance. Moderate innovation in all the pieces is the surest and easiest way to capture this style, because balancing acts (like juggling) can be tricky. On the other hand, perfectly executed balancing acts sometimes earn standing ovations.

RIGHT. The impact of this outfit comes principally from color, and that is what elevates it into the crisp mode. The windbreaker jacket is vibrant teal blue instead of more customary tan. The conventionally styled shirt is unconventionally striped in teal and mauve.

Another unexpected touch— though not an immoderately audacious one—is wearing the straight-necked, slightly textural lightweight maize-colored sweater under the shirt instead of over it.

The steel gray pleated pants also add a dash of innovation to convey crispness. Outfit (excepting sweater): Alexander Julian. Sweater: Float. Model: Peter Macci.

Although we're dealing with fine lines, doing so is important and imperative. Without making such distinctions, it's impossible for you to present traits distinctly in your garb. So, let's get down to a few more specifics.

GENDER BENDER

You learned in the first chapter that V-, Y- and T-shaped outfits are the sexiest because they are distinctively "male." Since these shapes signify manly garb, you do not want to abandon them entirely in your quest to display attributes other than sensuality. One purpose of any outfit is to establish beyond question the wearer's gender.

However, when portraying sexiness is not of utmost concern, there is no need to exaggerate the V-, Y- and T-shapes. In fact, the H-shape, which is unsexy because it fails to accentuate the male anatomy, becomes an acceptable shape to convey different characteristics. For example, a natural-shoulder suit whose coat has no waist suppression and whose trousers are straight-legged will impose an H-shape on its wearer, but if the suit's fabric is striped in innovative colors, the impression will still be crisp: the traditional cut of the suit establishes the necessary moderation, while the innovative coloration updates the suit's traditional associations. With a moderately innovative dress shirt and a moderately innovative necktie, the overall effect will be decidedly crisp.

Obviously, the same elements that affected a garment's sexiness will also affect crispness, so let's explore shape, texture, color and/or pattern and garment psychology in the light of crispness.

ABOVE. These two pairs of shorts are coordinated differently to show how crispness is achieved through a balancing of convention and innovation.

The white shorts on the right are very traditional. The addition of the innovative sweater—a brightly colored updating of the familiar Argyle pattern—turns the outfit crisp.

By contrast, the shorts on the left are themselves innovative by virtue of their roomier proportions. That's why the plaid shirt and cable-knit sweater selected are in the traditional vein. A more adventurous topping with these shorts would propel the outfit beyond crispness. Clothing (left, right): Robert Stock, Cesarani. Models (left, right): Patrick Taylor, Cameron Hall.

SHAPE

Since the crisp mode is rooted in convention, and since unusually shaped garb always clamors for attention (not a very decorous thing to do), only minor deviations from the traditional are allowable. Bell-bottom pants, for instance, would be entirely out of place, as would slacks with pencil-thin legs or zoot-suit pegged models. Extreme shapes are compatible with some other styles, but not with crispness.

TEXTURE

When you think of a crisp fabric, you probably think of a smooth one. Smooth textures and tight weaves are most compatible with the crisp style, although they're not obligatory. A burly cardigan sweater, for example, might be combined with a pair of chino slacks, an oxford button-down shirt and penny loafers to make a crisp impression . . . if the colors and patterns were balanced for innovative moderation.

Although the fabrics and textures most at home in the crisp school of dress are smooth ones, silks and leathers are exceptions in the major apparel pieces. (Silk neckties and leather shoes are fine.) A silk suit, for example, is too elegant to be categorized as crisp, and a leather suit is something else again. Generally, durable materials impart more crispness than novelties.

Consider it this way. What fabrics are used year in and year out in men's clothing? These fabrics, when colored and/or patterned correctly, should lay a solid groundwork for making a crisp impression. Ultimately, it's how every piece fits with every other piece that finally determines how successfully traits are conveyed. In the long run, only the total counts.

RIGHT. Although mostly associated with plaids, Madras fabrics also come in solids and stripes.

This Madras suit is very conventional in shape, but the emphatic stripes are not standard in natural-shoulder suits. Here the strength of the stripes is so innovative that overly adventurous colors would disqualify the suit from the crisp mode and push it into another realm. To keep this from happening, the stripes are in traditionally masculine blue and brown shades.

As assembled with the dress shirt and the pin-dotted tie, this outfit could be worn as on-duty garb, but it would also be more than acceptable for casually dressy social settings.

Replacing the shirt and tie with a polo shirt would make the outfit more definitively off-duty while still very crisp. Outfit: Cesarani. Model: Ken Batt.

COLOR

Color is the great separator, because it is so potent. Since the crisp style doesn't rely very heavily on garment cut to announce itself, nor does it ask much of textures other than that they be mostly smooth, the heavy load of identifying crispness falls to color.

Although most nongarish colors can be employed, the so-called masculine colors—blues, browns, greens—are among the most prominent, but usually in atypical versions to spark innovation. Yet, while the masculine colors predominate, occasional offbeat colors are sprinkled in to update the combinations. Since these out-of-the-ordinary color injections change from year to year, even season to season, particular combinations can't be specified. However, the general rule remains in effect without concession to time: the color base for the crisp style rests in masculine hues chosen to be somewhat unusual in their own right, while smaller doses of uncommon color that aren't traditionally considered truly manly fill out the crisp palette.

PSYCHOLOGY

While it's generally true that tampering with the basic integrity of a garment may pose problems, this is doubly so when you're attempting to convey crispness in your dress. Take a cardigan sweater, but a

BOTH LEFT. *The shapes of the garments shown are all quite traditional, and their textures are likewise on the typical side.*

Unusual color injections in the sweaters account for both outfits' crispness, since the pants in each are neutral, striped in gray and white. (On the far left, the pants are a seersucker material, which is strongly identified with the Ivy style; near left, the "chalk-stripe" pants are lightweight flannel.) In both instances, seafoam green and off-white are the principal colors in the sweaters.

Although green is traditionally considered a masculine color, the seafoam shade is not ordinarily used in menswear and therefore supplies necessary innovation to the outfits.

Additional innovation comes in two ways: in the outfit on the far left, the matched sweater set, joining a crewneck and a cardigan sweater, is noteworthy. Near left, the polo shirt, the ribbing of the sweater vest and the trousers are all striped in different scales for visual appeal often absent in more ordinary male costuming. Outfits: Ron Chereskin. Model: Joe Dakota.

RIGHT. *Madras plaids, part of the Preppy syndrome, are also highly visible in the crisp mode, although the garments cut from them often have distinguishing characteristics to set them apart from their purely Preppy counterparts.*

This shirt comes in an innovative magenta-and-chartreuse plaid. Also, in the Preppy scheme of things the shirt would likely have a button-down collar. Not this one. Here is a "pajama collar"—so named because it's the style commonly seen on pajama tops and not so commonly found on shirts.

Another innovative touch: the shirt pocket is cut on the bias and sparks interest.

Although the shirt cannot be considered radically dramatic, it is seemingly minor details such as these that all add up when you're putting an outfit together. Shirt: Robert Stock. Model: Rich Olsen.

fairly unusual one: it is long enough for the bottom to come to twelve inches or so above your knees, and the texture is very fuzzy. Such a sweater is no longer just a cardigan; it represents a hybrid between a sweater and outerwear (akin to a car coat). The psychology of the garment dismisses it from the crisp mode because this sweater-jacket is fundamentally too untraditional.

By comparison, most Madras garb automatically fits into the crisp classification, since Madras is associated with the Ivy style of the 1950s and '60s, and today's crisp style is a spinoff of that look. Still, although the crisp style does have similarities to ubiquitous Preppy, it avoids the clichés of Preppy outfitting by refusing to be predictable. The crisp Madras, for example, is generally colored in unconventional (but not too vibrant) hues. The psychology behind the Preppy style is, by adhering strictly to a proven formula, to validate one's social status by wearing a highly ranked, socially approved costume. At base, the crisp style is a repudiation of that manner of dress, because the whole point is to outfit oneself with some innovation and *not* to adhere to a proven formula. While the Preppy mode extols clannishness and implicit snobbishness, the crisp style celebrates the individual above the group.

ONE ON ONE

Since the primary thrust of the crisp look comes from color, and since the colors employed are constantly changing, don't expect any radical discoveries in this quick rundown of how certain styles in each of the various clothing classifications help transmit a crisp impression.

PANTS

In general, straight-legged trousers that fit the body comfortably but not tightly are a mainstay in the crisp mode. The male behind isn't obliterated, but it definitely isn't showcased.

In casual slacks, chino and khaki fabrics are preferred above denim. If denim is used, the pants should not be of the five-pocket Western-derived variety (typified by the famous Levi's 501 button-fly style). Instead, denim casual slacks should exhibit a fairly dressy cut.

In dress trousers, both pleats and cuffs are optional. The slacks may be somewhat wider in the thigh, but not exaggeratedly so. Gabardine is an often-used material, as is lightweight (not heavily napped) flannel. Pocket treatments tend toward minimalism, with only slits to reveal the pockets (and perhaps a discreet flap to cover the slit) as opposed to pockets that are sewn onto the surface of the trousers and therefore are much more prominently on display. Crisp garb almost always stays on the subtle side.

SHIRTS

As mentioned, oxford button-down-collared shirts loom large on the crisp scene, as do knitted polo shirts. They aren't obligatory, though. What is obligatory is that the shirts look neat, that they neither cling to nor balloon out from the torso, that they appear comfortable and not restraining in any way. Solid colors are typically pastels or midtones but seldom densely dark. Interesting stripes and small checks and plaids are often used. Sometimes the surface can be slightly lustrous, but not (as with satin garments) sleekly shiny. Only minimal surface textural interest is evident.

SWEATERS

Sweaters play a major role in the crisp style because they infuse outfits with unpredictable color and because they add softening textures that are usually lacking in the other garments. Sweater vests are especially welcome. Although solids can be utilized, the sweaters are often designed with contrast ribs around the neck and waist, and with other colorful details as well. Argyles are a favored motif, but in uncommon interpretations.

Subtle mixing of two or more patterns is a sophisticated ploy in the crisp style, and sweaters offer strong assistance by acting as buffers between patterns that might clash without separating referees. For

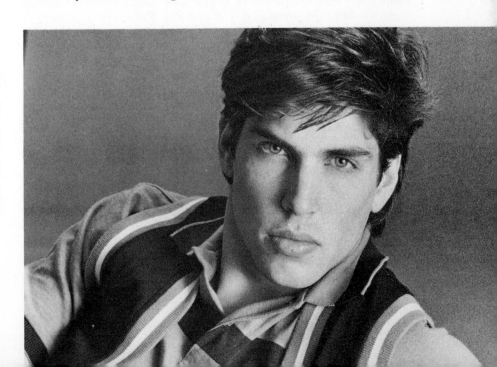

example, imagine an outfit made up of the following two pieces: tan trousers striped with pale yellow, mint green and raspberry, and a plaid shirt with an off-white ground, the bars of the plaid in the same hues as the trousers' stripes.

As presented, although the trousers and shirt are color-coordinated, they could look belligerently fussy together. Although there would be no color clash, the patterns might be too combative to be pleasing. However, if a sweater were added to separate the aggressive pattern combination, visual peace would be restored.

A solid V-neck in chocolate brown could do the mediating, but it would not be a particularly creative solution. What about a mint green V-neck sweater with two rows of stripes in pale yellow and raspberry along the V and around the cuffs and waist? That would be a more creative—but risky—solution. The danger? When colors coordinate exactly from piece to piece, the overall effect can be overly contrived. In this instance, coloring the sweater in a heather blend of the mint green and a warm tan would eliminate part of the problem and would impart some unpredictability. Although the sweater acts as a foil, it also makes a contribution of its own, and transforms the outfit into a crisp one.

SUITS

In its essential form, crisp off-duty garb gravitates toward the type of clothing that is sometimes found in on-duty outfits. Oxford-cloth button-down-collared shirts, for example, are very much at home worn with a business suit, and the straight-legged pant style most associated with off-duty crispness is also a style of pant seen in many on-duty suits. Because of this underlying linkage, dressy off-duty outfits (for dining out or attending the theater) can be expanded to bring in

ABOVE LEFT. Dressing down a suit is a crisp thing to do. This traditional pin-cord suit is treated untraditionally by placing of a textured T-shirt beneath it and scarfing the neck, thereby transforming the suit into off-duty or weekend gear.

Today many designers are creating what they call "weekend suits," most of which are lightweight versions of conventionally styled "workday suits." Suit: Cricketeer. T-shirt: Float. Model: Michael Principe.

ABOVE RIGHT. Sport-coat ensembles in the crisp mode often have more tactility than less dressy crisp outfits do to help maintain an off-duty feeling.

The dress shirt here is on the formal side, but the textural sweater and the tweedy jacket counteract its on-duty implications.

Bow ties, particularly when donned for pleasure, are strong on crispness. Here, because the tie has a limited number of stripes on a mostly solid ground, its pattern coordinates pleasingly with the striped shirt, especially since the collar is white. Outfit: Robert Stock. Model: Noa.

sport-coat ensembles. (If a suit is selected, make it fairly conventional with a dash of innovative accessorizing—say, a colorful shirt and an unusually patterned tie—to bolster unpredictability.)

Sport coats are more highly individualized than suit coats. Their textures and patterns can be much more adventurous, since they are spared the responsibility of matching trousers. Although crisp garb isn't noted for its tactility, nubby and tweedy sport coats are compatible if the other garments remain principally smooth. A silk necktie and a starched shirt, for example, are crisply worn with a nubby sport coat and gabardine or lightweight flannel slacks. However, the tactile qualities of a knit tie and corduroy pants would deny a crisp impression.

Sweaters and sweater vests are often combined with sport coats and neckties to downplay the on-duty connotations that might creep into the outfit without them.

A necktie and a sweater can sometimes replace a sport coat in the crisp sphere. Say you're attending a brunch given to introduce visiting parents to a small, select group of friends. You conclude that a suit is too formal for the occasion. You toy with wearing your gray herringbone sport coat, a blue crew-neck sweater (with a white shirt sans necktie beneath it) and dark blue gabardine slacks. That outfit would certainly be socially correct—though unadventurous and definitely not crisp. But you discover that your sport coat is at the cleaners'. When you add a cable-knit V-neck sweater in an offbeat shade of lavender and a silk tie striped in mauve, indigo and silver, you make a stylistic switch. The result embodies as much respectfulness as the sport-coat ensemble exhibited, but it adds a crispness

ABOVE. Although sporty in nature and origins, this outfit is crisp in the way it modifies the athletic components.

The shorts are styled like gym shorts, except that they're made of a woven, not knitted, material. The tank top has fine vertical stripes, as most truly athletic ones don't. The shirt is worn as a casual jacket and owes nothing—certainly not its little print or pajama collar—to sports gear.

Also, pastel yellow appears in all three garments. These modifications account for its crispness. Outfit: Ron Chereskin. Model: Patrick Taylor.

OPPOSITE PAGE. Woven swimwear with interesting patterns—such as the tropical-fish design on these trunks—falls into the crisp mode.

How clothing is worn can alter its impression. Here the message of the untied drawstring is sexy, not crisp: it subliminally tells onlookers that a gigantic effort would not be required to slip the trunks off.

With the drawstring tied and tucked inside, the trunks would be more clearly crisp. Some observers might prefer the first tale. Model: Russell Henis.

that the original outfit lacked. You are now presenting yourself as the imaginative fellow you are.

But occasionally suits are a part of the off-duty scenario. These are suits with a difference: they aren't primarily intended for on-duty use. Sometimes called weekend suits, they are most often created with lightweight fabrics, sometimes even of shirting materials. Their designers intend them to be play suits—not for infants, but for grown men who want to dress up in a relaxed, casual way. These new creations slip easily into the crisp mode.

SHORTS

Per usual, walking shorts high on visual stimulation (excepting unpredictable color) don't fit into the crisp genre. Bermuda shorts are the standard of moderation and thus represent the epitome of crisp shorts. Gym shorts made of pant fabrics (such as khaki or twill) also fit into the crisp mode, but nylon or knit gym shorts don't.

SWIM TRUNKS

Woven swimwear—as opposed to the stretchy type—is part of the crisp style, particularly when patterned. Skimpy or voluminous swimming attire is banned. But truthfully, conveying crispness is probably not uppermost in your mind when you slip into swimwear.

SLEEPWEAR

Transmitting a crisp image via sleepwear probably isn't your foremost burning desire either. If you're interested, cotton pajamas in a soft pastel hue are crisp sleepwear. A crisp robe is simple and ordinary, one without gimmicks.

FOOTWEAR

Tasseled leather loafers are a very crisp shoe style. They look equally good with dressy and fairly casual components. When an outfit is very casual, sailing shoes—often called by the registered name Top-Siders—in colors other than brown are a good choice, as are non-clunky sandals. Espadrilles—those rope-soled canvas knockabouts—are another. Of course, shoe styles are not confined only to these choices. In general, to impart the right feeling, shoes should not look as if they were selected strictly for their utility. Heavy soles, for instance, look very serviceable—occasionally too serviceable to be truly stylish. Crisp shoe styles should have a refined air. By their nature, most boots are more earthy than refined.

Since unpredictability is at the core of the crisp style, unusually patterned and colored socks do their bit.

OUTERWEAR

Although the crisp mode is far from casual, its appropriate outerwear is far from dressy: an overcoat style called a balmacaan. It is usually made of a rough woolen tweed and has raglan sleeves—slanting from under the armholes up to the collar line in front and back. When unbuttoned, the collar looks like a large-sized, open-at-the-neck shirt collar.

Okay, this coat isn't strictly crisp. For one thing, the texture is more tactile than that of most crisp fabrics. For another, it's fairly earthy. But to look for a purely crisp topcoat isn't really sensible. If you were to follow the guidelines for the crisp style to the letter, you would

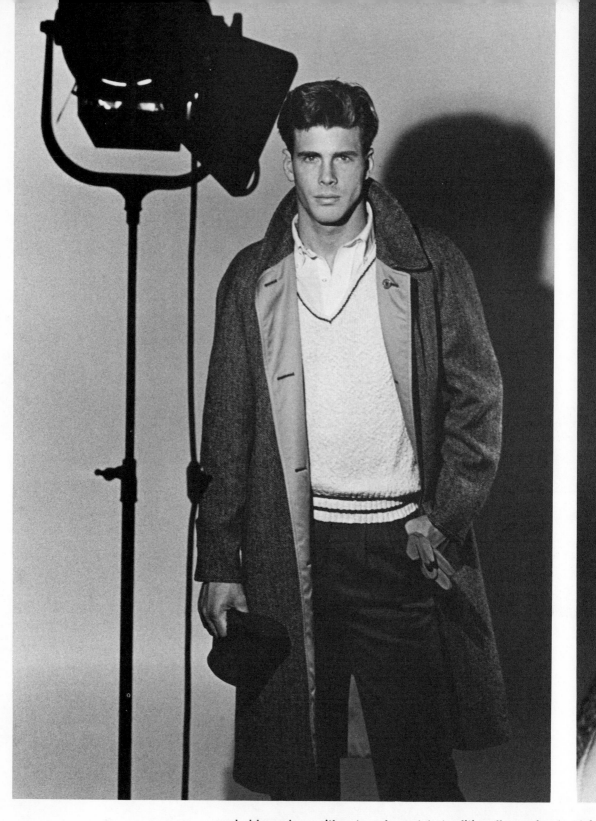

probably end up with a trench coat (a traditionally moderate style) colored in some uncommon way (to make it unpredictably innovative). Would you really want a pale celadon trench coat?

Since the function of outerwear is principally protective, it's sometimes wiser to adopt a nonspecific style than to pick out a garment so specific to one characteristic that you seriously limit its applicability for general use.

Tan windbreakers are staples in the male wardrobe, but interestingly striped or colored ones are not found in every quarter. Guess which ones are crisp.

Casual outerwear derived from sailing gear likewise does the crisp trick when colored contemporaneously.

Loads of pockets and zippers and paraphernalia are not part of crisp outerwear.

FORMALWEAR

You now know that moderate innovation is the hallmark of the crisp style, but for formal contexts, even moderate innovation can be too much. A white dinner jacket is technically correct evening wear during warm-weather months and on tropical cruises, but dark ones are more frequently seen. Thus, appearing in a white dinner jacket can be unpredictable enough. A double-breasted white dinner jacket is more unpredictable still. Wearing tartan formal trousers with a double-breasted white dinner jacket piles on extra innovation. A bright green bow tie and cummerbund could be pushing crispness to its innovative limit. You might defeat your goal of looking crisp by falling into the style called Smart! (Chapter 7.) But you needn't be dogmatic about perpetually projecting only one trait. In fact, you shouldn't be.

ACCESSORIES

To convey sensuality in your off-duty garb, you keep accessories to the bare limit. But to transmit crispness, you will reexamine the accessories' impact.

Caps and nondress hats spark interest, so they add a large dash of innovation to crisp outfitting, provided they're basically whimsical and not imbued with strong military connotations.

Colorful belts are effective, particularly in fairly dress-up situations. Tactically, they make it extra evident that the outfit is more than a minor rehashing of an on-duty uniform. In the same way, sporty watches offer more crispness than dress watches. Expensive-looking jewelry is a sign of conspicuous consumption, too heavy with the imagery of power. Diamonds are not a crisp male's best friend.

Given the choice, go for lighthearted accessories over serious ones.

BELOW. This easygoing outfit would not be very expressive minus the hat, worn solely for fun; the proof is in the nonserious, upturned brim. But with the hat, the outfit becomes whimsically crisp. Outfit: Ron Chereskin. Hat: Screaming Mimi's. Model: Brad Brown.

OPPOSITE NEAR RIGHT. Every garment in this outfit is traditionally shaped, but the colors are not conventional. In particular, the dusty rose sport coat is responsible for the aura of crispness, while the robin's-egg blue dress shirt provides the mandatory "maleness." Outfit: Jeffrey Banks. Model: Dan Cahill.

FAR RIGHT. Again, garment color, not shape, breaks with tradition to impart crisp appeal. In this instance, all the color innovation is found in the plaid shirt. Outfit: Alan Flusser. Model: Terrence Dineen.

BELOW RIGHT. Once more, color is why this outfit is crisp. As is customary in this mode, the fabrics are smooth and the cut of the garments conventional. Outfit: Alexander Julian. Model: Lou LaRusso.

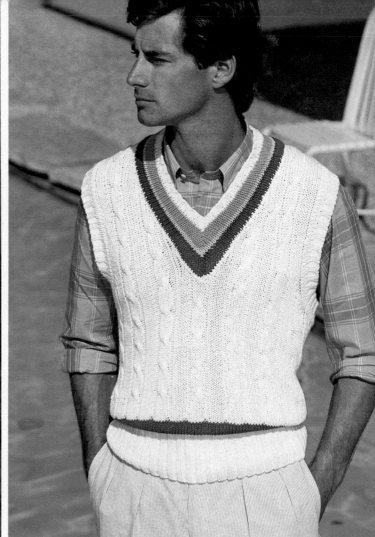
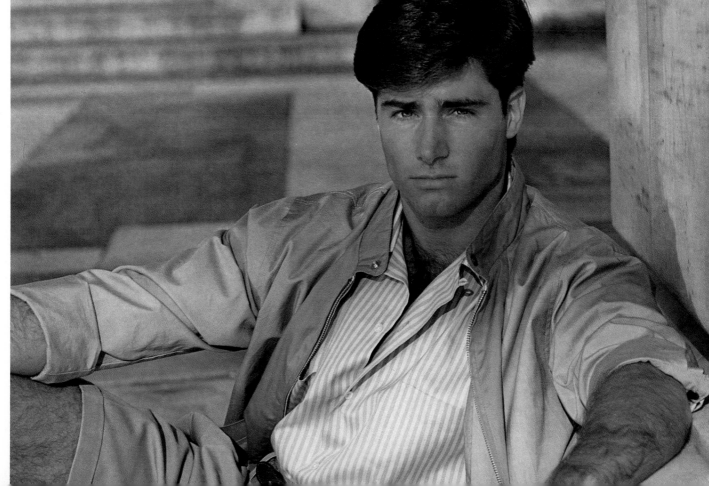

RIGHT. The clean, clear pastel colors in this conventionally shaped button-down-collar shirt set the scene for crispness, while the pale plum trousers almost push the outfit into a more innovative mode. Ultimately, it's the jacket that maintains the crisp aura. Not a standard style, the relatively short jacket, with V-notch lapels like the ones found on many traditional suit coats, buttons at the bottom the way many casual jackets do. The lustrous oyster collar has glints of pink and plum in a tactile weave. This is crispness at a highly sophisticated level. Jacket & pants: Ferragamo. Shirt: Alexander Julian. Model: Patrick Taylor.

LEFT. Here the same-colored stripes are found in both the shirt and the pants, but the shirt background is white while the trousers have a very soft blue-green background. Thus the stripes are more prominent in the shirt, so the outfit doesn't appear overly "mixed-and-matched."

The real focus of the outfit, of course, is the sweater vest with its multicolored cables winding up the chest. The hues relate to those found in both the shirt and pants, but the shades are brilliantly bright. Off-white frames the vibrant cables, providing visual relief. Outfit: Alexander Julian. Model: Gerald Tebo.

FOLLOWING PAGE, UPPER LEFT. This outfit evidences another crisp approach to color in conventionally shaped clothing. The stripes in the shirt are "jewel tones"—very rich, very bright, very intense—so dynamic that to remain part of a crisp outfit they need to be calmed down, balanced with less aggressive hues. The bouclé sweater vest supplies the necessary tranquillity.

The same colors found in the shirt appear in equal measure in the sweater, causing them to "blur." That accounts for the sweater's overall "grayed" cast, even though you can identify the individual jewel tones if you concentrate and try to single them out.

The pastel teal blue pants are coolly colored, so they also counteract the forward advance of the shirt. Outfit: Alexander Julian. Model: Lou LaRusso.

FITTING IN

Concerning universal acceptance, you're in a more favorable position if you dress to project a crisp aura than if your intent is to convey sensuality. But no manner of dressing can ever ensure universal acceptance. Don't expect clothing to perform miracles. But do expect clothing to challenge ingrained beliefs.

Since a measure of sophistication is incorporated into the crisp style, certain distrustful people will probably not fall sway to crisp imagery. Resistant to visual changes in the status quo, these people are the fashion conservatives who believe any deviation from the absolutely conventional suggests deviant behavior. What can you do when facing such pettiness? Ignore it. *You* know who and what you are; certainty of your self-worth should help you rise above prejudice.

How can you help eradicate clothing bigotry? By recognizing the social parameters of all occasions and then by dressing to please yourself within those confines. By presenting the *true* you to the fashion fascists in the world out there, and then by acting humanely. Since the *true* you encompasses several traits, when you dress in a nonstatic way you will be constantly reminding *them* that pigeonholes are for nesting pigeons, not for separating human beings. Dressing the free way means being free to be yourself, oblivious to small minds and small people. You may even convert some of those diehards. If you don't try, who will?

UPPER NEAR LEFT. *The shoes and socks both pick up the color of the pants in darkened variations to complete this outfit down to the final details, giving the fellow a crisp look from head to toe. Clothing: Alexander Julian. Shoes: Cesare Pacioti (exclusively for Wilkes Bashford in San Francisco). Model: Lou LaRusso.*

LEFT. *Interesting shoes tell observers where someone stands on the matter of clothing innovation.*

Bright green sailing shoes worn as street attire are a couple of long strides beyond the Preppy symbolism of brown or tan Top-Siders. Colorful high-top gym shoes prove someone is a sport if not necessarily a jock. Red-and-black shoes are funky and fun, though too flamboyant to aptly be called crisp. When business wing-tips are reinterpreted with checks and white laces, the break with convention is complete; they won't be passed by unnoticed.

By comparison with the other styles, fringed leather slip-ons seem sedate. In less colorful company, this last pair would look a step above most conventionally designed shoes.

The point is clear: clothing perceptions change whenever a great diversity of styles is in evidence. Here the most conservative shoes are "oddball," in the same way a man in a business suit looks out of his element at a costume party. Shoes (left to right): Cole-Haan, Roger Forsythe, Vittorio Ricci, Vittorio Ricci, Cole-Haan.

CHAPTER 3
EASY!

PACIFIC OVERTURES

Maybe your mission in life doesn't include reforming the world's attitudes toward clothes. Maybe you have little or no inclination to thumb your nose at fashion conservatives. You don't yearn for sartorial finesse. You simply want to put your off-duty garb together with a minimum of hassle. You don't expect or ask your clothes to make huge philosophical statements about who you are.

Your clothing will make statements about you even if that's not your intention. If your major wish is that your clothing speak softly—so that you'll appear to be a soft-spoken, easygoing guy—most of the time you'll be predisposed to a style called Easy! (If that's how you want to appear some of the time, you'll gravitate toward this style when you want.)

Easy clothes—like easy guys—don't make waves (or very rarely do) and don't go against anyone's grain (well, hardly anyone's). They're nice, and everyone (well, almost everyone) likes them. Lacking the assertiveness to want to be leaders, easygoing fellows are usually wary of heading the parade, and easygoing clothes usually, though not necessarily, lag several steps behind fashion trends.

Since the easy mode is so easy to understand, deciphering it will not be complicated.

SHAPE

The cut of garments is conventional, not at all innovative. Shirts button straight up and down symmetrically, for instance, and they all come with collars, except when they're T-shirts—in which case the T-shirts have round necks, not atypical V-shaped ones. Ordinary shapes prevail.

LEFT. Easy clothing is in some ways similar to sport apparel because of the "brotherhood" of uniforms. In the easy mode, however, it's important that the donning of this type of clothing never appear to be an "offensive" tactic. When garb associated with any form of competition is adopted, it should be well worn, even frayed or slightly torn, to suggest it is past its prime and no longer to convey any hint of aggression. These gym shorts, for example, seem to be a relic of bygone days and therefore imply easy comfort, not a combative spirit. Model: Bryan Coolahan.

TEXTURE

Friendly imagery is central to the easy story. Previously we explored tactility in terms of sensuality, but soft textures are also friendly, because a pal never presents a forbidding facade. Think of it this way: an embrace can be erotic or it can be platonic. Soft-surfaced garb colored in nonsexy hues will emit friendliness, not sexuality.

COLOR

Untraditional colors have little place in the easy mode. Although an offbeat shade may make a fleeting appearance, more typically the palette consists of warm-hued neutrals—browns, rusts and greens—colors that are easily approachable because they're naturally outgoing. Blues are marginally okay, since they are so firmly believed to be manly, but (to repeat an earlier observation) blue also symbolizes reserve; a color that recedes isn't as friendly as an advancing one.

LEFT. Although the easy style is not noted for stylish innovation, it need not be totally bland. Short on drama, this warmly colored outfit is nevertheless very pleasant.

Although an easy impression would be possible without the sweater vest, it is the most important element in the ensemble, since its tactile texture advances like a welcoming handshake. Outfit: Jeffrey Banks. Model: Bryan Coolahan.

NEAR RIGHT. This outfit is the most graphic of the three depicted on this spread, but it manages to remain in the easy mode because it seems that no concentrated thought went into concocting it: onlookers assume the fellow is attired in this getup because each article was handy when he was getting dressed. This artlessness (whether true or contrived) is the hallmark of transmitting easiness.

Imagine a cap angled jauntily on the guy's head. That would destroy the whole illusion of easiness, since observers assume that caps—especially jauntily angled ones—are worn for purposeful effect. The easy style must appear to be effortless. Sweater: RGFM. Model: Tom Hill.

FAR RIGHT. Why do you think this fellow is wearing a tie? Do you suspect it's because he thinks he should, not because he particularly wants to? Do you know why you suspect this to be true? Here's why: the brushed surface of the shirt is warm and informal; so is the loose, tactile surface of the homey cardigan sweater; even the corduroy trousers suggest informality.

And what about the choice of the tie? It's an informal knitted one, not formal silk.

With so many elements conveying informality, it's next to impossible to believe this man would deliberately embrace the formality symbolized in a necktie, since all other indications are he's a very easy guy. Outfit: Ron Chereskin. Model: Terry Van Derent.

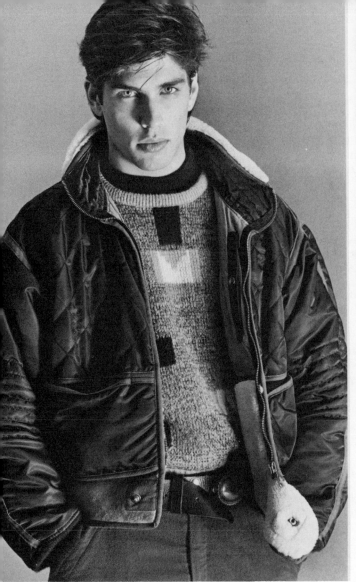

Plaids—especially plaid shirts in masculine, warm color combinations—are the easiest, friendliest patterns.

TEAM SPIRIT

Although uniforms deemphasize individuality, certain costumes promote geniality among those who wear the same uniform or part of it. The British are particularly aware of this, as evidenced by their fondness for the club tie, a long-established style first worn to indicate that the wearer had attended such-and-such a school, or belonged to this or that club. (A club tie has a repeating motif, such as small horseshoes or hunting horns or pheasants or you-name-it strategically placed on a solid ground.) Regimentally striped neckwear is also British in ancestry and was originally worn by British officers in mufti to indicate the regiment to which each officer belonged. In both these examples, the ties were created with the knowledge that clothing can establish positive links between people who may never have met but who will presumably be compatible because their backgrounds are similar. The ties also exclude those who aren't privileged to wear them.

Clothing can create a community of spirit among people who dress

ABOVE. "Club" ties have a buddy-buddy quality very compatible with the easy style of dress, so they are a good alternative to knitted neckties when ties are on the agenda for a social event. If you stare very close and hard, you may be able to pick out the horse heads on this necktie.

In keeping with the easy mode, this guy wears an ordinary button-down-collar shirt and conventional herring-bone-tweed jacket.

To show his friendly, nonaggressive nature, he has pinned a flower to his lapel. Jacket: Austen Reed. Tie: Celine. Shirt: Henry Grethel. Model: Lou LaRusso.

OPPOSITE PAGE. As noted, a sign of masculine camaraderie is evidenced by wearing part of a sporting uniform, since team sports are high in the mythology of good-fellowship—toward one's team members if not the opposition.

So that those without team connections won't interpret the clothing as aggressive, it's better if a sporty garment is oversized or beat-up or both if you want to project easiness. When you want to exhibit vigorous physicality, sport clothing should flatter your physique, not hide it. Model: Nelson Gonzalez.

similarly, because a kindred taste in clothing presupposes a kindredness of spirit. Conversely, when people dress very differently, they will probably unthinkingly be wary of each other, because the dissimilarity of their attire intimates disparity in their backgrounds or views. Facing such an array of clothing styles, the participants unconsciously keep up their defensive guards in case hostilities should erupt.

The easy style of dress is steeped in familiarity and therefore tends to dissipate the potentially aggressive reactions of others by pacifying their fears of the alien. Machismo has no place here, nor does any claim to physical superiority, because both can be threatening. Obviously, none of the hallmarks of the sexy mode are applicable: sexiness arouses emotions, doesn't becalm them. And the colors of the crisp mode are too adventurous: adventure involves danger. At its philosophical (and behavioral) base, the easy look displays bonhomie to prove you're one of the boys, and a good guy to boot.

The easy style is not "proper," because stiff correctness implies too much reserve, in the same way that someone who speaks with perfect grammar is often thought of as stuffy. Continuing this analogy, the easy style is colloquial. Not vulgar street talk. It's slang without any curses.

PLAYING AROUND

In recent years, clothing that was once worn for sports—warm-up suits, tennis togs, gym shorts, jersey T-shirts—has increasingly hit the streets as casual gear. In the language of the fashion industry, such garb is called sportswear, sometimes activewear. A relatively new fashion category—spectator sportswear—encompasses sporty clothing that isn't durable or sturdy enough to withstand the rigors of athletic activity but that has enough "sportiness" in the design to bring sports to mind. A jacket that vaguely looks like a baseball jacket but really isn't one, for example, falls into the spectator-sportswear department.

These arcane distinctions have a point. Since strong physicality can project a bravado at odds with the easy style, clothing that's emphatically athletic is too showy (figuratively and sometimes veritably) to fit in. It stands out too much and also calls too much attention to the body (sometimes by revealing it). Spectator sportswear, by contrast, recalls the chumminess of enthusiasts gathered together to watch an event without pretending they have the physical prowess to take part in the real game. Thus, spectator sportswear is nonaggressive and gregarious: it's easy.

Since most true sportswear is body-conscious and therefore more sexy than easy, the way to turn it into easy apparel is to eradicate body-consciousness by wearing purposefully oversized sporty garments. Minus shoulder pads, a football jersey droops without a hint of menace.

(For those times and situations when you want to show off your body and appear athletically Sporty! check out Chapter 6.)

BEAR HUGS

You've seen it on the football field, when the victorious players all but render themselves insensible whomping one another's backs as they clasp each other in viselike grips. The bear hug is the supreme sym-

bol of masculine camaraderie (and one of the few ways society allows men to touch; they hug but don't kiss).

Although the easy style is not at all pugnacious, it nonetheless is definitely manly. To maintain its masculine aura, it draws heavily on the principles of group identity. To be Good-time Charlie on the campus, dress like the other Good-time Charlies. To be Average Joe in the office, dress like the other Average Joes. To be Mister Good Guy at the picnic, dress like the other Mister Good Guys. And so on. Even in clothing, imitation is a sincere form of flattery and sometimes the ticket into the group.

So what are the garments that have passed the test of time to proclaim conventional masculinity? We've already listed them in the Crisp! chapter (2). As you recall, to appear crisp, you color traditional garb with moderate innovation. To relax and take it easy, you need never nod to innovation if you choose not to. Instead of mustard chinos, you can wear tan ones. Why look for a mauve button-down-collared shirt when you can get by with your light blue one?

Of course, when you are wearing only the most conventional of conventional attire, you will probably be overlooked in a crowd. That's okay sometimes. When you're in the bleachers watching a

LEFT. Large-scaled plaid flannel shirts suggest the affability of easy-going lumberjacks. One style of very textural, neutral turtlenecks goes by the name of fisherman's sweater and likewise conveys man-to-man friendliness. There is an earthiness to these garments, and in some instances wearing them together will suggest an earthy nature, not necessarily an easy one.

Here, however, the flannel shirt—worn as a shirt jacket—is colored pale purple and peach. Since these are not earthy colors, they dispel any overriding impression of earthiness and instead project easiness with a touch of innovation.

To be less innovative—and easier—the plaid would come in warm, masculine hues. Shirt: Ron Chereskin. Model: Joe Kloenne.

RIGHT. Sweaters are widely worn in all the off-duty modes. When you combine a fairly conventional sweater with rather ordinary pants, the effect is generally an easy one.

Here neither the sweater nor the corduroy pants are innovative, and the outfit has no extra fillip to distinguish it. From a stylistic viewpoint, the child's fur cap is the most imaginative garment in sight, causing the man's outfit to recede, provoking little if any interest. Clothing that is this nonassertive is definitely easy. Model: Joe Dakota. Child: Troy Brown.

baseball game, feeling one of the crowd (at least of the crowd rooting for your favorite team) is part of the experience, part of the enjoyment. After all, easy garb does prove you're one of the boys.

Although boys will be boys, on occasion you will want to prove you're your own man. This is not easy in the easy style, but it's possible. To show you how, let's rummage among three garments drenched in easiness and splash them up a very little bit.

THE SEERSUCKER SUIT

This long-established summertime style with its characteristic crinkled stripes has been a mainstay in the male wardrobe for decades. The usual—easiest—way to assemble a whole outfit is to add a white button-down-collared shirt and a navy blue silk necktie. An alternative shirt is pink instead of white, and the navy blue silk necktie becomes a knit. That's it. Nothing painful. And the impression is still one of ease. If you puff a maroon-and-blue printed foulard square into the coat's breast pocket, you're dangerously close to exiting easy territory, but it's doubtful you'll be gunned down because of the trespass.

97

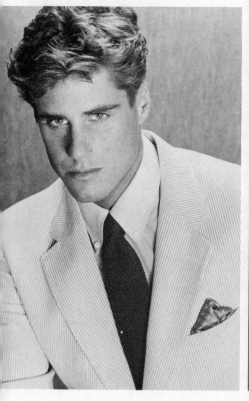 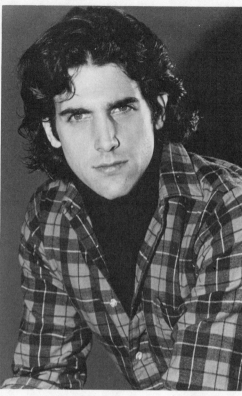 

(By the way, foulard prints come in infinite variety, but are mostly based on small geometric or amoebalike forms.)

THE FLANNEL SHIRT

Snug and huggable flannel shirts are very easygoing. Those made of tartan plaid are usually worn with loose jeans or tan corduroy pants. How about exchanging the tan corduroys for steel gray ones? Nothing flashy, just a hint more dapper. But you won't lose your easy membership card.

(In case you didn't know, the clans of the Scottish Highlands design and weave their own distinctive plaids—more properly called tartans —to signify kinship. The clans look poorly on outsiders' appropriating their tartans. Nowadays, the term tartan plaid is used generically, just as glen plaid—the type traditionally found in some suitings—is also a generic term.)

THE CARDIGAN SWEATER

Who said that only navy blue cardigans are easy? A chocolate brown one with pale yellow-and-cream striped ribbing is no less comfortable and no less easy, but definitely more friendly and certainly not flamboyant. You can still wear it with khakis. You could even put a tattersall-check shirt beneath it without shocking the world or your bosom buddies.

(FYI: Tattersall checks are regularly spaced overchecks framed by horizontal and vertical stripes that generally come in two colors and

ABOVE LEFT. Since easy outfits purposefully avoid making large statements, whenever you try to make them appear more exciting you risk making them appear too exciting, no longer easy. A little detail—placing a small-scaled patterned silk square in the breast pocket of the seersucker suit coat—raises the outfit above the mundane. Suit: Cricketeer. Model: Peter Macci.

ABOVE MIDDLE. Plaid shirts are very easygoing and are often called "work shirts." They remain easy, but less workmanlike, if you simply wear a turtleneck sweater under them for an extra iota of style. Model: David Hocs.

ABOVE RIGHT. A pinch of spice can be added to easy cardigan sweaters when they have something "extra," such as collars. Instead of the standard flannel shirt, one with an interesting check adds visual appeal without pushing an outfit beyond easy limits. Sweater & shirt: Robert Stock. Model: Pat Hardie.

appear on a light-colored background. They are often used in dress shirts. In fact, you could even add a rust knitted necktie to the reassembled outfit for casually dressy occasions.)

DOWN UNDER

If you enter a room and conversation stops so that the crowd can crane its collective neck to study your garb, you are not dressed in the easy style. Every garment should have an aura of familiarity about it. Any deviation from the norm is minor, never major. Understatement is the key. In some cases, this means dressing at a level below the crowd's expectations. For example, a man lacking a dinner jacket of his own and the funds to rent one could improvise a formal look by wearing his classic blue blazer, gray flannel slacks, a white shirt, a tartan-plaid bow tie and a matching cummerbund. Fashion snobs will look down their noses, but less persnickety types will recognize that the outfit represents a sincere attempt to live up to the spirit, if not the formal letter, of the event.

This last distinction is the last word about the easy style. It should never be slovenly or boorish. It should never be viewed as rude or rebellious. Although understated, it still must make an attempt to approximate the etiquette of the situation. You must use your common sense to determine the dividing line between appearing comfortably easygoing and contemptuously underdressed.

RIGHT. Take a close look. Don't be deceived by the bow tie and cummerbund. That is no dinner jacket. The man is wearing a conventional blue blazer and gray flannel pants, even a white button-down-collar shirt.

The only formal ingredients are the silk bow tie and cummerbund, and they happen to be in a deep blue, dark green and maroon plaid.

This is one of the easiest ways to satisfy the requirements of a "Black Tie Optional" event when you want to make a special effort but choose not to go whole hog. This outfit would be wrong for a "White Tie" event calling for strict dress protocol.

When clothing requirements are stringent and you don't feel like meeting them, you can always exercise your option to stay home or go to the movies instead. Blazer, pants: Austen Reed. Tie & cummerbund: Christian Dior. Model: Stuart Carberry.

CHAPTER 4
EARTHY!

TOP SOIL

The easy mode was easy to dissect, but more multifaceted is the style called Earthy! It's not always simple to capture or to carry off, and just as there are many ways to dress to convey sexiness or other qualities, many are the ways to appear earthy, some more markedly so than others. But once you've dug in and learned the lay of the land, you'll see how the unpretentious, uninhibited, worldly, hearty, sometimes even bawdy, qualities of the various earthy looks can be irresistible to some, perhaps objectionable to others. Not everyone considers the earthy style worthy of cultivation. So be it. After all, in some of its guises, we are talking about an uncommon style that's for the uncommon man. In other manifestations, it is very common. Too common, some say.

Color is the main determinant. In most cases, earth colors—those found in nature, in the soil and in foliage, including the spectrum of browns, oranges and greens—predominate. Splitting hairs, gray, being neutral, is seldom considered an earth tone, although certain shades of gray can fall into the category when the right conditions are set.

NATURAL ACTS

LEFT. Earthiness is not the easiest trait to describe. When you see it, you recognize it. Here, for instance, since camouflage prints are very dominant (more about that later in this chapter), the major impression is an earthy one, although a sexy intent is also evident. Of course, earthiness and sexiness are often—though not always—closely aligned: earthy clothing covers a wide range. Shirt: The Trader. Model: Chris Doyle.

Time for some more color theory.

When natural light passes through a crystal prism, it is dispersed into eleven "pure" colors: red, red-orange, orange, yellow-orange, yellow, yellow-green, green, blue-green, blue, blue-violet and violet. In nature, red-violet is missing from the light spectrum, but it is added as a basic hue to round out the number of pure colors to an even dozen.

Among these pure colors are the so-called primary, secondary and intermediate colors. Red, yellow and blue are the three primary col-

101

ors—the most purely pigment-saturated of all, and the ones from which all other colors are produced. Equal mixtures of each two of the three primaries produce the three secondary colors: orange, violet and green. A mixture of a primary and a secondary color yields an intermediate color—red-orange, yellow-orange, yellow-green, blue-green, blue-violet or red-violet.

Tertiary colors are mixtures of the secondary colors and can be mixed with one another or with any other hues to create new colors. On an artist's color wheel, literally hundreds of hues are positioned side by side to show what shades are produced by a mixing of equal amounts of adjoining colors.

When the twelve pure hues are spacially positioned in a circular relationship, the three primary colors are located equidistant from each other, as are the three secondary colors. Falling between the primary and secondary colors are the six intermediate colors, likewise equidistant from each other.

Analogous colors are those which appear side by side. For example, five analogous colors centering around blue-green are yellow-green, green, the central blue-green, blue and blue-violet. In their pure forms, analogous colors are always harmonious, particularly so when close to each other. Thus, while blue-green and blue-violet are harmonious, yellow-green and primary green are even more harmonious because of their closer proximity. When colors are closely related by sharing the parentage of a single color, they get along easily without apparent friction: shades of yellow combine more harmoniously—and restfully to the eye—than combinations of yellows and blues.

Complementary colors are direct opposites. Some opposing pairs are yellow and violet, blue-violet and yellow-orange, red and green. These warm/cool duos always contrast. Although complementary colors don't clash—after all, opposites attract—their union is never as peacefully harmonious as the coupling of analogous colors. Pure complementary-color combinations are dynamic and forceful to the eye. Whitened or darkened complementary-color combinations, though less assertive than the pure ones, retain a degree of assertiveness.

As you know, shades of red and yellow are warm, advancing colors while blues and greens are cooler, more receding. But green hues, because they include yellow, are relatively warmer than blue hues.

When you want to break down the reserve of cool colors, warm colors must be introduced. In fact, warm colors appear even warmer when contrasted with neutral or cool hues. For example, yellow and red—both warm colors—look equally warm in combination with each other. But when you put red next to static gray, the red appears warmer and more advancing than when paired with yellow, because together the red and yellow compete for attention, and neither gains the upper hand. When a warm color is joined with less aggressive hues, though, it easily claims the greater attention. Thus, small touches of warm color can make more of an impact than their size might suggest.

The intensity of a color also affects the way it acts. Pale yellow advances more than dark blue. But pigment-saturated pure blue actually advances more strongly than pale yellow. Intense colors, then, even if nominally cool, are more visually advancing than very whitened or very darkened warm colors. On the other hand, when you compare several deep and dark shades with a collection of assorted soft and light shades, the paler ones advance more than the dark ones. Dark colors are always the most recessive, while intense colors are the most advancing. The most advancing intense colors are the pure warm hues.

Most earth colors don't fall into the primary, secondary or intermediate ranges; they are mixtures of several colors. In value, they are more often darkish than lightish. For earth colors to warmly advance, they require a fair share of either yellow or red in their shadings to combat the recessive nature of darkish hues. Rust is a very warm earth color because it contains, in addition to earthy brown, strong doses of red and orange. Olive drab is a less warm earth color, because, although it too contains earthy brown, the other main ingredients are green and yellow, but not red. Intermediate orange—the equal mix of primary yellow and primary red—is the warmest of the earth tones—much warmer than intermediate green, which is strongly infused with blue.

MIX MASTERS

Despite the seeming complexity of color, there are only three fundamental methods for using it in your clothes: you can employ color monochromatically, analogously or complementarily.

With the monochromatic technique, all the pieces in an outfit are either the same color (such as the exact same shade of blue) or in the same color family (for instance, different shades of blue). Very earthy is a monochromatic outfit in, for example, various shades of green.

The analogous technique combines colors that are close relatives, but not from the exact same color lineage. Brown and green are analogous colors and earthy too, so an outfit composed of shades of these two colors is therefore also earthy, but no more or less earthy than the one of monochromatic green.

The complementary technique, by contrast, partners colors from contrasting color families. Green and orange are earthy, contrasting colors, and an outfit containing only shades of green and orange is earthy in the assertive complementary way. But it isn't more or less earthy than the other two. Bear in mind that earthiness is a very versatile trait.

Monochromes, which transmit only one color message, are very definitive. A monochromatic red outfit makes an emphatically impassioned appeal. By comparison, most earthy monochromatic outfits, though emotional, are not so overt.

Analogous colors make less direct statements, because more than one color message must be deciphered. However, since analogous colors are closely related, analogously colored outfits are tension-free and clearly free of ambivalence. Most analogous earthy outfits are discernibly warm in sentiment.

Because complementary colors are always based on warm-cool contrast, they are the most complex in their pronouncements. The internal tension among the colors doesn't necessarily suggest combat, but outfits colored complementarily are never serene. The apparent conflicting color message is akin to a cryptogram that can require skillful decoding. Thus, complementary color schemes are often more cerebral than emotional. Because of their complexity, they can be very intriguing. When made up of tertiary colors, complementaries can be downright mysterious or exotic. When the color scheme is extremely intricate, they can be absolutely puzzling, but far from dull.

In the earthy mode, you can use color in any of the three ways—monochromatically, analogously or complementarily. When every article of clothing is one shade or another of brown, the earthy impression is straightforward and uncomplicated. Shades of brown combined with analogous shades of rust and orange are earthy as well, but the impression is now warmer, more intimate and emotional. Should you inject a contrasting pale blue-green shade into this last color scheme, the overall effect will still be earthy but not quite as warmly so, because now the color combination is more complex, has greater warm-cool tension. Now the effect has become more cerebral, its emotionalism lessened.

GROUND LEVEL

Although earth colors are the harbingers of the earthy mode, let's not forget that earthiness has some "coarseness" to it—coarse fabrics, that is. These fabrics are more "natural," less "refined," than smooth fabrics because of the way they're woven.

In technical parlance, wool (or wool-blended) fabrics are either worsted or woolen. Worsted fabrics are made of worsted yarns—firm, strong, smooth-surfaced yarns spun from combed wool—as opposed to woolen yarns, which are fuzzier and softer because the wool is not combed prior to being spun into yarn. Woolen fabrics are more "natural," less "refined"—literally coarser. This coarseness adds to their earthiness. Certain fabrics with names like cheviot, herringbone and hopsacking are inherently more earthy than smoother twills, chinos and sharkskins. But don't worry about learning the names; just check their surfaces to determine whether fabrics are earthy or not. As a point of reference, it's difficult to conceive of a tweed fabric that isn't earthy.

The shape of clothing has little to do with its earthiness. (More detailed information about this later.) Garments can be cut in an avant-garde manner, for instance, and if the requisite colors and textures are found among the individual pieces, the impression will be of earthiness plus iconoclasm—the look of a dedicated adventurer. On the other hand, if garments are cut in a very traditional way, with the individual pieces all properly colored and textured, the impression will be of earthiness plus civility—the look of a prototypical country gentleman.

LEFT. This jacket is especially earthy because the fur suggests a trapper wearing his spoils on his back. Jacket: Egon von Furstenberg. Other clothing: Charivari Workshop. Model: Chris Zambelli.

RIGHT. This burly, roomy zip-front sweater (layered over another sweater) is heavy enough to serve as outerwear, and colored earthily enough to carry the entire load for projecting earthiness. Sweaters: Basco. Pants: Samuelson & Abrams. Scarf: Susan Horton. Model: Neil Kramer.

PAGE 106, TOP RIGHT. The tactility of the tweed sport coat works as a softening agent to eliminate strict business connotations and starts the outfit on the road to earthiness. If you look very closely, you will notice a faint bronze "windowpane" plaid superimposed on the fabric. This color is picked up in the pigskin vest, also tactile. But the main contributor to the earthy impression is the orange-and-gray-green plaid shirt. This outfit is in complementary colors. Model: Robert Dahlin.

PAGE 106, BOTTOM LEFT. Here is another complementarily colored earthy outfit, based principally on green and red-orange. The fairly large pattern on the sweater coordinates with the fairly small scale of the stripes in the shirt. The colors in the sweater and shirt also coordinate well, since the same colors in only slightly different shades appear in both. Because blue—not an earthy tone—appears in both the sweater and shirt, this outfit has more advancing-receding internal tension than many earthy ensembles do. Outfit: Missoni. Model: Todd Bentley.

PAGE 106, LOWER RIGHT. Another example of complementary colors in the earthy mode. The olive green jacket roots the outfit in earthiness, but only barely. If the paler olive hue didn't appear in the striped shirt, one wouldn't call the total earthy, since neither lavender (in the striped shirt) nor turquoise (the color of the sweater worn under the shirt) is an earthy color. Yet turquoise is a mixture of green and blue, plus white, so it is distantly related to earthiness through the green. Jacket and shirt: Alexander Julian. Model: Peter Macci.

OPPOSITE FULL PAGE. For the moment, overlook the gray-and-orange plaid shirt worn under the sweater. Without it, this outfit would be monochromatically conceived, since it then would be composed almost exclusively of neutral shades of gray. Now reinsert the shirt. That touch of orange—the warmest earthy color—turns the outfit into a truly earthy one.

Technically, because of the orange shade, the color combination should be called a complementary one. However, since the orange is minimal—though exceedingly important—one might stretch a point and say this is basically a monochromatic outfit. Jacket & shirt: Robert Stock. Sweater: Peter Barton's Closet. Model: Gerald Tebo.

PAGE 108, TOP LEFT. Because tactility suggests earthiness when the colors don't interfere, the blocks of green in this very fuzzy sweater help to place it in the earthy category. Another prominent hue is indigo-purple, so the sweater's color combination is complementary. Sweater: RGFM. Model: Chris Zambelli.

PAGE 108, TOP RIGHT. This earthy outfit is dressed up with a white shirt and a tie, but earthy it remains since the major components are earthy brown. Though dressy, it's also very warm and advancing because of the red belt and tie. Clothing: Basile. Model: Todd Bentley.

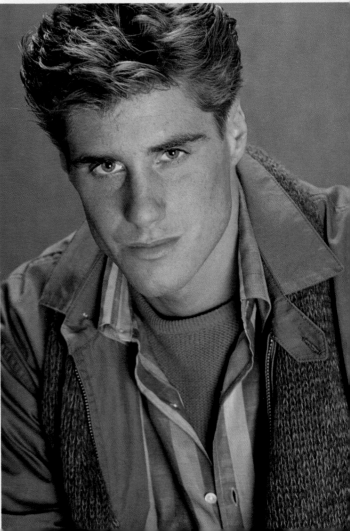

BELOW LEFT. Even in a city park, this outfit smacks of the countryside. Tweed sport coats are inherently more outdoorsy than flatter, smoother ones.

Since yellow is infused in both the forest green of the turtleneck and the bronze corduroy pants—both of which are markedly tactile—this outfit is analogously colored and therefore more harmonious than the three complementarily colored outfits shown on page 106. Outfit: Cesarani. Model: Ron LaRussa.

BELOW RIGHT. Duffel coats like this one evoke thoughts of a brisk stroll

outdoors, so they are particularly earthy when colored in an earthy hue.

Donegal-tweed pants like these with tactile slubs of color appearing randomly in the weave have a "coarseness" that is also very earthy.

Sweaters that look hand-woven suggest the rural craft of a cottage industry with an implicit closeness to nature.

The addition of a bow tie doesn't disperse earthiness, only elevates it to the imagery of a country squire. Clothing: Alan Flusser. Model: Mateo.

Since earthiness can be expressed in diverse ways, it is rarely an appropriate or an inappropriate style in and of itself. Its "correctness" or lack thereof stems from the cut of the garments, and how appropriate to the situation those shapes may or may not be. For example, sexily shaped clothing can be colored and textured to project earthiness along with sexiness; conventionally shaped clothing can also be colored and textured to project earthiness along with conventionality. Where sexy outfitting is acceptable, so are sexy outfits in earthy colors and textures; where sexy outfitting is unacceptable, earthy colors and textures won't change the fact. Ditto for conventionally shaped clothing.

The earthy mode can be highly sophisticated or simply rustic. At its best, whatever the form of expression, it remains approachable and very personal.

PLAIN FOLK

By virtue of living off the land, some people are reputed to be virtuous because they "have their feet on the ground." Farmers, ranchers, lumberjacks, foresters—these are among the ostensibly hardworking individuals who have the inside edge on being "the salt of the earth." Their figurative and literal proximity to the soil and all things natural is reflected in the simplicity of their garb, which never evidences highfalutin airs: finery is for city cousins who've forsaken their roots and possibly their souls through the seductions of high living.

Although tillers of the soil have no claim to sophisticated style, their "plain folk" reputation endows their clothing with positive merit. The earthiness of their garb is associated with trustworthiness and decency.

Because this attire is unequivocal about its modest roots, by nature it's at odds with the cerebral complexity of complementary colorations. However, the warm-cool tension of complementary earthy colors will elevate the down-home connotations of the garb, make it spiffier. So will offbeat accessories, such as a Navajo belt or a finely feathered headband on a felt cowboy hat.

GOOD DEEDS

While scraping out an existence by tilling the soil is supposedly good for the soul, one isn't necessarily penalized for success. Positive associations also surround the landed gentry who haven't lost touch with the good earth.

The romance of the country squire and the manorly, mannerly gentleman bespeaks clean air and fertile fields. The vice and corruption of the city are far away in distance as well as mind. Although the country gent's wardrobe is less rudimentary than the homely garb of

ABOVE LEFT. This loosely woven shirt looks "primitive" enough to bring to mind native crafts and therefore suggests earthiness—literal closeness to the soil and one's roots. Model: Lazaro Felekis. Styling by Angelo Droulia. Photographed on the Greek island of Mykonos.

ABOVE RIGHT. Bib overalls conjure up thoughts of farming and the positive virtues of tilling the land, so they are automatically earthy; and strong plaids recall hearty, earthy lumberjacks. Outfit: Basco. Model: Cameron Hall.

RIGHT. More sophisticated earthiness is suggested by the tweedy "country gentleman" look, which can range from lived-in scruffy to dressed-up spiffy, provided the textures are mostly tactile and the colors strongly earth-related.

Here the body of the cardigan sweater is brown suede, while the ribbing and arms are knitted brown with colorful slubs.

The nap of the plaid flannel pants is pronounced, to increase the earthy appeal of the outfit. Clothing: Robert Stock. Cap: Michael Stromar. Model: Joe Dakota.

BOTH RIGHT. Sometimes one garment is so strongly identified with a particular style of dress that simply wearing it is sufficient to convey a specific trait.

In this case, the British-in-origin tweed topcoat is fraught with manorly connotations that convey earthiness.

Note the collar which, when buttoned, resembles a shirt collar, as opposed to the lapeled collars of more formal outerwear. This relative informality, characteristic of the balmacaan coat style, adds a feeling of warmth to the "country gentleman" imagery.

As it happens, the tactile scarf and sweater are colored in earthy tones to compound earthiness, but even when they're not visible to onlookers, the coat alone transmits earthiness. Model: Bryan Coolahan. Styling (also page 114): I Love Ricky.

112

his tenant farmers, it is still handsomely homey, as opposed to sleekly citified.

This dimension of the earthy mode is laced with nostalgia. Little rational argument can be presented to make a case for the perpetuation of the country-gentleman look on urban terrain, other than the fact that it's rich in tradition and lore. Like farming gear, all tweeds and woolens evince some earthiness, but of a more "civilized," less "crude," type: they are worn to survey the ground, not to work it.

The civility of the country-gentleman look stems from its long association with the British aristocracy. Therefore, it cannot create any highly visible breach with conventional shape. The colors and textures of this clothing always mirror the rural *land*scape, never mean streets. Although monochromatic and analogous colors can be used, complementary hues are more pertinent, to reinforce the impression that the squire has made a conscious decision to embrace rusticity and isn't stuck in the hinterlands against his volition: he has enough panache to make it in the city but *chooses* the gentility of country life.

ROAD WAYS

The mythology that those who live close to the earth are more worthy than those who sweat it out in mechanized industry is so ingrained that even the rootless existence of nomadic foragers has romantic, earthy connotations.

Traveling the earth with no home base, rovers are true backpackers: all they own they carry on their bodies. An earthy representation

LEFT. Here the same topcoat seen in the preceding double-page spread is worn with dramatic flourish off the shoulders as a cape with an imaginatively woven sweater. The layering effect suggests the nomadic life, conjuring up earthiness. Sweater: G. Maislinger. Model: Bryan Coolahan.

RIGHT. Sometimes an itinerant earthy look stems from military gear, which often serves as inspiration for off-duty garb.

Since military imagery can be both sexy and earthy, and since sexiness is a more dominant trait than earthiness, military-derived clothing tends to look sexy rather than earthy. Adding an unsexy newspaper boy's cap, work boots and suspenders here helps reduce sexiness and advances earthiness more strongly. Outfit: Charivari Workshop. Hat: Screaming Mimi's. Model: Neil Kramer.

of the nomadic lifestyle is found in the dressing technique called "layering"—wearing layers of several garments when a lesser number would probably do. For instance, a layered outfit can consist of a turtleneck sweater worn beneath a plaid shirt worn beneath a V-neck sweater worn beneath a jacket, plus obligatory trousers, shoes and socks. Such an ensemble is high in protective warmth, but the same amount of protection can be afforded by fewer garments—by a down-filled, quilted parka worn above a turtleneck sweater worn above obligatory trousers, shoes and socks. However, the layered outfit is earthy and the parka outfit isn't necessarily so. Layering carries with it the vestigial sense of the foraging life and consequently conveys earthiness.

Layered clothing can be colored monochromatically, analogously or complementarily, although complementary colors in abundance can suggest the shiftlessness of gypsies. Understated analogous colors are more inherently respectable when the pieces are many.

DRUM BEATS

Big-game hunting is high adventure, man against the wild. Despite valid environmental concerns, romance still surrounds the safari, and safari outfits have earthy appeal. So does most survival gear—a rugged earthiness that works best when textures are flatly resistant to abuse and when colorations are monochromatic, especially in the tan hues.

Military attire connotes a different type of survival. Its styling, like that of safari gear, is highly distinctive, with a plentitude of pockets.

LOWER LEFT. Military-inspired clothing also conveys adventure, particularly so when camouflage prints—originally created as a protective design to make the wearer "disappear" into the foliage of the countryside—are part of the costume. On urban streets, camouflage prints confound their original purpose and cause you to stand out in the crowd. A sense of aggression definitely remains. Coat and pants: Ron Chereskin. Shirt: The Trader. Model: David Hocs.

LOWER RIGHT. Safari styling projects the macho side of earthiness. To cut down the inherent aggression of safari clothing, you can select a jacket

in an iridescent fabric instead of more typical, lacking-in-luster twill, and add garments not in the safari vein. Outfit: Ermenegildo Zegna. Model: Terry Van Derent.

RIGHT. Clothing styles that aren't inherently earthy can assume earthy overtones when they are properly hued because earthiness is essentially a matter of color.

Since this ensemble—which exhibits no recognizable earthy origins—is composed totally of pale earthy shades, its effect is distinctly earthy.

In vibrant colors, the outfit would not convey earthiness. Outfit: Ferragamo. Model: Tom Tripodi.

In the face of adversity, men wear uniforms to endow them with courage that otherwise they might lack. The power of the uniform is primitive and superstitious and formidable. Subliminally, safari and military costuming has nearly enough earthy strength to equal that of highly dominant sexy clothing. Sexy clothing is potent with passion. Safari and military clothing is naturally engorged with passion of a different sort: the relentless need to triumph through sheer guts.

LUSH LIFE

Although clothing suggesting a livelihood close to the earth subconsciously implies earthiness, an outfit can be earthy without such associations.

At first this may be confusing, so concentrate.

Imagine a conventionally shaped gabardine business suit in dusty blue worn with an ecru combed-cotton shirt and an orange silk tie. Not earthy, is it? However, if the dusty blue suit were of a coarsely woven hopsacking fabric, if the ecru shirt were of napped brushed cotton and the orange silk tie were a nubby knit, then the ensemble would exhibit some earthiness, because now the tactility of all the textures suggests earthiness. Also, ecru is a faintly earthy color while orange is a very earthy hue, and the dustiness of the blue gives it a distant relationship to more legitimate earth tones. (Naturally, if the coarsely woven suit were recolored in a fir green shade, greater earthiness would be evidenced; but the geography of earthiness is not neatly mapped.)

Continuing with this point, imagine an outfit of all smooth textures

in very traditional shapes: a cornflower blue shirt, a coal black sweater and midnight blue trousers. Color-switch: now the shirt is tangerine, the sweater is roan brown and the trousers are sepia. Switch to earthiness complete.

Without affecting the color change, a retexturing of the original outfit into entirely tactile textures won't make it earthy, because the initial color combination is too antithetical to earthiness. In other words, earthy textures don't necessarily an earthy outfit make, but earthy colors do. In the best of all earthy worlds, both colors and textures are earthy to project lush earthiness.

LOOSE CHANGE

One style of off-duty dress is called Loose! (You'll be reading about it next, in Chapter 5.) Since the shape of loose clothing is proportioned more generously than is customary in traditional men's clothing, the statements made by garments in this mode are more pronounced than those of most other styles. Literally taking up more space, roomy clothes always receive greater attention. As a result, clothing in the loose mode, when colored earthily, appears earthier than similarly colored conventionally cut clothing. But large garments will transmit any quality, not just earthiness, with greater volume than traditionally shaped garb because of their greater volume of size.

Subtle monochromatic color is less blaring on loose clothing than intense complementary combinations. So are earthy analogous colors.

SHOW STOPPERS

Outfits can be highly innovative in literally thousands of ways, with earthy colors and textures utilized in many of them. However, whenever innovation is extremely evident in an earthy ensemble, or whenever a trait stronger than earthiness is manifested in the outfit, earthiness yields to that other show-stopping attribute. Sexiness, for instance, is a more dominant trait than earthiness. Consequently, a sexy outfit colored in earth tones and textured earthily remains predominantly sexy, secondarily earthy.

Similarly, clothing unusually shaped is inherently innovative, and as innovation increases, so does show-stopping capability. Therefore, even when a highly innovative outfit is colored and textured earthily, onlookers will react to it principally in terms of its innovation before registering its earthiness. And there's nothing wrong with that. An eye-catcher of an outfit that's earthy is anything but weak-willed, even when others respond more weakly to its earthiness than to its innovation. Should you want to give such an off-duty outfit a name, it is Smart! (Chapter 7.) As an on-duty outfit, it would be Ingenious! (Chapter 10.)

UNDER WRAPS

Overlapping exists, as is evident, between the various modes, including the off-duty and the on-duty categories. After all, earthy colors and textures are found in all types of gear. Remember that fact when you enter Part II (On-Duty Garb), especially when you encounter the mode called Ingenious! Meanwhile, as a respite from the occasional murkiness of the earthy style, hang in there and proceed to the next chapter, where you can hang Loose!

CHAPTER 5
LOOSE!

TIME CAPSULE

Although there are ongoing principles in menswear, clothing is not static. Most notions about why fashions change are, to put it bluntly, bull. One of the most widespread misreadings is the conspiracy theory—that clothing designers and manufacturers are in cahoots with each other, scheming together to make this year's fashions outdated next year so we'll all spend our hard-earned bucks on new duds annually to replace our obsolete ones.

Since so many people believe in the conspiracy theory of fashion change, let's take a few minutes to prove it false.

First, clothing designers, rather than being in collusion, are fiercely jealous of each other and try to be as secretive as possible about their work to keep others from stealing their ideas. Every designer of note—and every designer aspiring to become noteworthy—attempts to come up with new items to capture the fancy of the consuming public. This is doubly true of designers who produce expensive clothing, since they know that the majority of people do not buy extremely high-ticketed clothes. Rather than joining together to foist unwanted fashion on an unknowing public, designers are driven, like all other businesspeople, by the profit motive, and they compete with each other ruthlessly.

Second, if the conspiracy theory were correct, only one type of clothing would ever be available at any given time, and what is available one year would be vastly different from what was offered the last. But this is hogwash. A tremendous variety of clothing styles are always on the market, from the very traditional to the futuristic. In fact, many designers produce several collections of clothing at various prices to offer greater choice. Many manufacturers do the same. One giant suit manufacturer, for example, markets more than a dozen brand names in styles from traditional American to experimental European.

LEFT. Loose clothing is just what the phrase connotes: loose in proportion, although some articles are more ample than others. The garb also expresses a looseness of outlook—a deviation from conventional attitudes.

The crinkled fabric of this roomy shirt is a visual repudiation of the "starched-shirt" syndrome which symbolizes the business of business. That it is worn completely unbuttoned is likewise a total departure from the norm.

The pleated pants are full in the thighs and also send out loose signals. Pants: Alan Flusser. Model: Robert Henry.

Third, even if a conspiracy were afoot, it would be a pretty harmless one, since the buying patterns of most men are not greatly affected by changes in so-called Fashion. Except for the relatively small number of individuals hooked on Fashion, most adult males gravitate to one style of clothing only and stick to it, with minor variations on that look, from year to year.

Fourth, the conspiracy theory underestimates the common sense of the average individual. For the conspiracy theory to work, the public would have to be basically mindless, placidly awaiting manipulation. Few people are that easily brainwashed.

Last, the conspiracy theory is illogical. The automobile industry isn't criticized for bringing out new models every year, and not everybody buys a new car every twelve months just because styles change annually. It is standard business procedure to introduce stylistic changes in everything from toothpaste packaging to television antennae. If fashion did not change, people would feel frustrated. Even people who rarely purchase clothing seldom want to buy exactly what they already own. Utter uniformity is utterly undesirable.

Fashions change because people want them to. When it sometimes happens that several designers introduce similar styles at the same time, this is not evidence of a cabal. What it does prove is why successful designers are successful—because they have an intuitive sense of the times and can predict what new styles people will want to wear before people realize it themselves: good designers are attuned in ways that ordinary people are not.

Fashion designers are interpreters, not dictators or conspirators. They translate sociological currents into clothing styles. Traditional designers create for traditionalists, but according to the current

ABOVE. There has been a recent influx into the American market of Japanese designs. Characterized in many cases by oversized proportions and intricate workmanship, these creations have been very influential in high-fashion circles . . . even though in Japan there has been an ongoing fascination with traditional American fashion in the Ivy League mode.

Although often difficult to decipher, fashion changes generally reflect sociological change. These two highly styled outfits, for example, though they may seem exaggerated to some, look less bizarre today than if they had appeared a decade or two ago.

When they did arrive, the name of the Japanese designer who conceived them was virtually unknown to American consumers, so the impact of the style could in no way be construed as proof of a "designer conspiracy." Outfits: Matsuda. Sunglasses: Ray-Ban. Models (left, right): Richard Villella, Jhamil.

RIGHT. Many of the recent largely proportioned garments have been so

122

mood of traditionalists. Avant-garde designers create for more adventurous sorts, but avant-garde expressions change with the mood of the times.

It is *we* who cause fashions to change because we're human. Sometimes we're dissatisfied with the way the country is being run, so we vote in new leaders. Sometimes we tire of the same old food and frequent new restaurants. Sometimes we become bored with the way we look and embrace new clothing concepts. Clothing, like the rest of existence, is always in a state of transition. Some people and institutions change more rapidly than others. Similarly, some people are more amenable to fashion change than others. But changes in fashion, though sometimes fanciful, are seldom irrational. As we ourselves change, we redefine our existence. Clothing change is part of that process.

ALTERNATING CURRENT

Lacking the feeling that their lives have fallen into an unalterable course, the young are often more receptive to shifting clothing styles than the elderly. The young are also more susceptible to fads; it's as if they were trying on new personalities when they outfit themselves

roomy that at first glance one might assume the intent to be a purposeful obliteration of body form. On closer analysis, however, one may discover that the intent is to exaggerate body proportions to overstated grandeur.

This boxy vest, although it does dwarf the man's actual chest, suggests the chest dimensions of a demigod. The shirt and pants are likewise commodious enough to accommodate superhuman musculature.

The dramatic proportions, however, are not accompanied by a highly dramatic pattern mix. Imagine the cut of the garments to be conventionally smaller. Then these patterns —a solid vest, a medium-scaled striped shirt and mini-checked pants (so mini, in fact, that the pants almost appear to be in a solid fabric)— would likewise seem quite conventional.

It is the largeness of the garments that accounts for the largeness of this outfit's impact, not highly innovative patterns, and certainly not emphatic textures, since all of these are smoothly flat. Clothing: Armand Diradourian. Model: Blake Dawson.

in new ways in quick succession. Their experimentation with clothing parallels their experimentation with life itself.

Not surprisingly, fashion change occurs much more rapidly among the young. They are also fashion's leaders, the testers of what might eventually reach mass popularity among older people as well. Certain styles are designed with the more receptive young in mind. In the language of the men's-fashion industry, this is "forward" fashion, and its target market is men in their late teens, twenties and thirties. These males are also more likely to have bodies that look good in "forward" styles.

Until relatively recently, most forward male fashion was very body-conscious. Designer jeans, the rage for several years, were about as tight as tight could get. Form-fitting shirts accompanied butt- and thigh-clinging jeans. Then, what amounted to a fashion revolution occurred. Although tight designer jeans didn't disappear—they're

LEFT. *Since large shapes make large impressions, they can suggest large egos. Here the large shapes are combined with very dark colors to make the impression even more imposing.*

The medium-toned graphic sweater dissipates the strength of the outfit somewhat and avoids a menacing appearance by softening the color scheme and adding tactility.

In design conception, the outfit is totally conceived, with piping both along the panel insets at the sleeves and down the sides of the pants; the vertical stripes of the belt echo the vertical ribbing at the neck of the sweater. Clothing: Charivari Workshop. Model: Todd Neuhaus.

RIGHT. *With only the jacket in a dark color, this outfit appears less "aggressive" than the one just discussed, even though the proportions of the two are very similar. The dark jacket does add more authority, however, than if it were colored in a pale, advancing hue.*

The color scheme as employed is intriguing, almost mysterious, because onlookers can't be certain of the true intent: as noted, the jacket color suggests serious reserve, while the earthy neutrals in the sweater imply approachable warmth. The dusty pink pants are not simply emotional because they've been muted with gray and in fact are even piped down the side and detailed near the fly with a truly gray shade. (Gray is basically close-mouthed in communicativeness.)

Although the outfit's message is not readily apparent, the largeness of the ambivalent statement demands that onlookers make their own decision about its meaning.

Most likely, because the pants are the most intriguing aspect of the outfit, and because of the fly detail, a loose interpretation will be that sex looms large in this person's outlook. Jacket and pants: Bech Thomassen. Sweater: G. Maislinger. Model: Benjamin Hobbs.

PRECEDING DOUBLE-PAGE SPREAD. The outfit evidences only slight ambivalence. The prominent rich blue-purple color of the shirt is lustrously mysterious, but that's the color selected to run down the crotch of the pants, otherwise mainly—and graphically—striped in darker, more neutral tones. The message? Lusty sophistication on a big scale. Clothing: Andrew Fezza. Model: Joe Kloenne.

LEFT. Although white is associated with purity, all is far from pure here. Notice the two mesh tank tops worn under this white jumpsuit telling observers to check out what's under them. This is no retiring wallflower. If more proof is needed, look at the belt wrapped twice to decorate the body, not to secure the garment. Belt: Robin Kahn. Model: Jhamil.

BOTH RIGHT. The larger the pattern and the looser the garment, the more impact loose garb has. Here the sweater is not dramatically bigger than many conventional ones, but its chevron pattern increases its apparent size.

Similarly, the pants are not as roomy as many, but inset panels of twill material at the sides contrast with the wide-wale corduroy to add extra dimensions.

Loosely proportioned off-duty pants are emblematic of the loose mode of dress because symbolically and literally they mark a departure from the blatant sexuality of designer jeans. Model: Pat Hardie.

still around—forward fashion became roomier, more amply proportioned. A new style was born, one named Loose! This style is still only in its early evolutionary stages.

Viewed in historical perspective, the loose mode was inevitable in its coming. Tight, body-conscious clothing came to the fore during a period when sexual mores were in transition. Discos were an all-consuming addiction, and sexual freedom was a comparatively new idea. Males and females were openly on the make, and permissiveness reigned. Sex clubs advertised in the Yellow Pages. Clothing was a self-admitted, self-advertised come-on.

Reaction set in. With everybody struggling to get into the tightest clothing around, suddenly a new style of looser apparel looked more tantalizing.

What's important to keep in mind about the foregoing discussion is that this new apparel was a repudiation not of looking sexy, but of looking sexy in what had become a commonplace way. Thus, a new style was inaugurated to look tantalizing in a new way. And it was a very particular style, not at all tentlike, to draw attention to the body

LEFT. Linen and linenlike fabrics that wrinkle are widely used in today's loose mode. Wearing two loose shirts, one atop the other as a shirt jacket, even when indoors, is another standard ploy.

Pale neutral colors are often the basis of those ensembles, because most neutral shades coordinate easily with each other. In fact, the paler neutrals are, the more likely they will go well together, especially with injections of white creating common bonds.

Here, although the overshirt is striped, the stripes are light-colored and thus the pattern is not emphatic; the overall effect is restfully harmonious. Notice that the overshirt is collarless, which makes it combine readily and noncombatively with the small-collared shirt beneath it. Outfit: Ermenegildo Zegna. Decorative fabric (right as well): Lee-Jaffa. Model: Charlie Melite.

RIGHT. Here the colors are darker than in the outfit just discussed, but since they're in similar noncontrasting value, they also combine harmoniously.

Because the knitted tank-top-inspired shirt is oversized and worn with nothing beneath, it reveals more than it conceals.

Imagine this outfit colored in two different ways. First, see it in shades of slate gray. Next, pretend that the top is red trimmed in yellow-orange and the pants are emerald green.

Obviously the second colorway is more dynamic—possibly too dynamic and forceful for an outfit already forceful in its roomy dimensions.

Strong color comes on very strong in loose clothing and should be chosen with discretion; at an intimate gathering, brilliantly hued loose outfits can storm the atmosphere. Clothing: Parachute. Model: Brian Terrell.

by mixing exaggeration with subtlety. Although the newly styled pants in the loose mode were—and are—wide in the thighs (exaggeration), they were—and are—shaped to show the male behind without overtly flagging attention to it (subtlety) the way designer jeans do.

The tightness of designer jeans was stylistically on-target for the prevailing sociological mood when they were first shown. If today's pants in the loose mode had been introduced at that time, they would probably have flopped—commercially as well as literally. But in the current climate, they are right, because the current national mood is an antithesis of the singles-bar syndrome. Although we still seek sexual gratification, sex today is seldom viewed as an end in itself. Having experimented with open sexuality, we learned the emptiness of sex without caring. Now, while the importance of sexuality hasn't diminished, sex is seen as a component of commitment. To use a clichéd expression, "me" has become "we": the Me Generation is now seeking an ongoing relationship, wants more than a one-night stand. Designer jeans symbolized fast and facile sex. You have to look more closely at today's sexy loose pants to discover their sexuality, just as you have to examine strangers more closely when you entertain the possibility of becoming a couple, not merely of coupling.

Designer jeans haven't yet become totally passé, and maybe they never will, since for many, jeans are a way of life. But designer jeans no longer epitomize our sexual culture as graphically as pants in the loose mode do.

HANGING OUT

The loose mode extends beyond one style of pants. Larger proportions are also found in sweaters, shirts, outerwear, you name it. Accompanying the looseness of shape is a looseness of attitude. A loose person isn't uptight about formalities or about courting approval; someone who's loose first pleases himself and is far from wretched if he displeases someone else in the process. A rebellious streak is fermenting beneath that loose facade, and it's not truly hidden: desirous of making a bigger-than-life impression, the loose individual exposes the fact that he expects to claim the lion's share of what life has to offer and that his appetite isn't easily sated by the conventional. Because the loose mode employs overstatement and enlarges apparent physical dimensions, it contains elements of aggression.

To reduce what might be interpreted as a menacing threat, loose clothing is often colored in neutral hues and textured tactilely. However, neither neutral colors nor tactile textures are indispensable. Rudimentary are the large proportions and nothing else. Different facets of looseness are communicated by different colors, textures and patterns.

COLOR

As just noted, neutral colors tame some of the aggressiveness of the loose mode because they indicate that the wearer is in a neutral stance, not on the offensive. Black tends to be even more sinister than usual in loose garb, unless a large amount of another color is combined with it. White apparel in the loose mode assumes greater purity and therefore is very pacific.

Primary and other pure colors advance all the more when they're found on large shapes, so they announce their individual color messages with great emphasis.

Loose outfits in complementary color schemes can be overpowering, because the automatic internal tension of complementary color combinations can appear almost explosive in big color blocks. Naturally, the brighter the complementary colors, the greater the apparent nervous energy. Greatly lightened or darkened complementary colors are less contrasting and consequently less aggressive in appearance.

Earthy colors are that much more earthy when they're given more room for visibility.

In general, whatever colors do under other circumstances they do with extra measure when they're on extra measures of fabric.

TEXTURE

As with colors, so with textures: the basic nature of an individual texture is intensified when given more room to make itself known. Hard textures look more rigid than ever in the loose mode, and soft, emotional ones seem softer and more emotional. For this reason, to give loose outfits some balance, textural contrast is often advisable. Smooth leather pants, for example, are often worn with tucked-in-at-the-waist draping shirts in a typical loose look. Given the roomy proportions of the garments, exclusively soft textures are seldom used, because a womanly impression might be made.

PATTERN

Solid colors are more central to the loose mode than a mixture of several patterns because with this scale of clothing, several patterns in concert would be startling. When pattern is used, most likely it is large-scaled and on only one garment. On the other hand, color bands—a stripe of contrasting color around the neck or across the shoulder of a jacket or shirt, for example—are prominent on many loose pieces and often take the place of repetitive patterns.

END ZONES

Since the loose mode is fairly new to the men's-clothing scene, it's too soon to predict whether its effects will be long-term or short-lived. As presented here, the principles of the style are reasonably stringent. However, expect to see modification over the years, if the style lasts for years. Already some loose pieces are being combined with garments of other modes to make a more eclectic statement. And already stylistic flourishes from other modes are being adapted to the loose imagery. Rather than seeing this as a bastardization of the mode, recognize that clothing that doesn't change is suitable for museums. Also, remember that you can always have your own input into the development of your clothing, since new styles arise out of existing styles. An inert mode is a dead end.

BOTH LEFT. This outfit is not truly characteristic of the loose mode, even though all the garments are amply proportioned, and therefore pose unusual considerations.

First, take the matter of the over-shirt. It is very strongly patterned, but in checks—a fairly common motif in male patterns. Consequently, though large, the pattern is not greatly aggressive because it is very familiar. However, this is a black-and-white check, and no two "colors" are more diametrically opposed than black and white. (Technically, black and white aren't considered colors, but let's not get bogged down in technicalities.) As a result, the overshirt demands attention because of its strong black-and-white contrast but doesn't command attention for very long because of the familiarity of the checked pattern, large though it may be.

Second, consider the tank top. It's striped, and quite strongly so. But the stripes arise from textural, not color, contrast, since the top is white with alternating tightly woven and loosely woven vertical bands.

Third, the neutral beige clamdiggers are loose in the crotch but tight in the thighs.

In theory, this outfit should not work because, again theoretically, the two shirts, given their roomy dimensions, are too strongly patterned to be worn together. (In more modest cuts, there would be no problem.)

Also in theory, because the clamdiggers shift abruptly from roominess in the crotch to tightness in the thighs, they should be stylistically inconsistent with the tops. But they're not.

Almost inexplicably, the outfit does work, but on its own terms: since it is so casual, the type worn totally for play with no pretense of any seriousness, wide berth is allowed.

That the colors are neutral black, white and beige also helps. In vivid, hot hues, the effect might be clownish. But clowns are playful, so in play clothes, anything goes.

What's wrong in theory can look right in practice when you take the experimental plunge. Overshirt: Enrico Coveri. Tank top & shorts: Float. Model: Doug Spitz.

CHAPTER 6
SPORTY!

STREET TALK

That clothing designed for sport activities is now worn as casual gear is not a new phenomenon. In fact, a great quantity of clothing currently considered dressy started its life as, first, sport apparel and, later, as casual dress before its elevation. Today's top hat and tails, for example, ascended to the height of formality after shedding their humble origin, during the middle of the eighteenth century, as clothing intended solely for horseback riding. The progenitor of today's business suit—initially called a lounge suit because men "lounged" in it—was originally created for watching sports and was therefore considered too informal to be taken seriously in the business milieu. Sport coats are called sport coats because, in the early decades of this century when business attire was highly formal, a gentleman played tennis or softball or other sports in a *sport* coat.

After World War I, and particularly after World War II, the distinction between sport and casual clothing became more and more blurred. At the same time, dress clothing became increasingly "sportier," and what had formerly been considered off-duty garb began to be seen in on-duty situations. The ongoing movement in menswear has been toward more relaxation and greater freedom. Once, even the boys working in the mail room of newspaper offices wore suits; today, by-lined reporters often wear jogging shoes and sweat shirts on their beat. Generally, however, only individuals involved in menial labor, in factory work or at lowly echelons can get away with wearing sport clothes as work attire, because sports smack of leisure and play, not the grind. By and large, authentic sport clothes—ones that can actually withstand the rigors of the wearer's participating in an actual sporting event—remain off-duty garb except for professional athletes.

The allure of big-time sports is one of the major reasons sport

LEFT. Some authentic sport clothing may be designed to protect the body, but more often the intent is to make the body look aggressively forceful.

Wearing sport apparel—whether the real stuff or garb derived from a sporting activity—can lessen one's individuality in favor of imaginary identification with a triumphant team. Model: John Burke.

clothing is so popular. Children often dress themselves in the team uniform of their favorite heroes without realizing that this form of imitation parallels the primitive notion that by donning another's clothing one magically assumes the powers of the clothing's owner. Similarly, many adult males aren't consciously aware that they often wear sporty garb to capture for themselves the physical and emotional excitement of sporting activity without undergoing the disciplined training required to be a successful athlete. Many of these men are also blind to how strongly charged sport clothing is with aggression and sex.

GAME PLAN

If some people hope to win heroic attributes by imitating athletic dress, the primary goal of many team uniforms is to win through intimidation. Sport uniforms—even those for nonteam activities like

ABOVE. The phrase ski sweater brings to mind a wide range of bulky sweaters that may never see the lodge. And so-called ski jackets are favored outerwear anywhere when the thermometer dips.

Although the wearing of actual ski gear like that shown here would be considered odd away from the slopes, imagine the outfit minus the goggles and poles but with a pair of corduroy pants. It then becomes highly acceptable and dramatically visible, imbued with the romance of the sport. Outfit: Descente. Model: Tom Tripodi.

OPPOSITE UPPER RIGHT. Uniforms for rough-and-tumble team sports are often designed with stronger graphics than clothing for less vigorous activities. Those for hockey, for example, generally employ bolder colors than baseball uniforms, symbolizing increased danger.

Perhaps because hockey is not as popular a sport as baseball, hockey has seldom been an inspiration for casual clothing styles, whereas variations on baseball jackets and caps have been popular with many non-players.

This sweater with crossed hockey sticks inset on the chest could easily be taken from the "activewear" camp (as shown) and combined with casual slacks—about the only way to bring the tumult of hockey into street fashion. Outfit: Robert Stock. Model: Pat Hardie.

tennis, boxing and swimming—are often emblazoned with stripes. Bright primary colors likewise generally embellish competitive garb. Although team uniforms tell to what side a player belongs, the real reason for all those stripes and brilliant colors on football jerseys (to choose the most obvious example) is to make the players look bigger, to exaggerate their physical dimensions through optical illusion. The stripes and brilliant colors represent physical challenge, an attempt to frighten the opposition into submission before combat begins. This is the same reason boxers enter the ring in robes to knock your eyes out.

But sport uniforms are more than bluff. By exaggerating the brute strength of the wearer, sport clothing plays up the body's physicality as well, thereby emphasizing its manliness. As a result, sport garb is sexy as well as aggressive—*not* because aggression is synonymous with sexiness, but because strong bodies are associated with strong sexuality.

Consider other ways sport apparel calls attention to the maleness

FAR LEFT. *In very casual settings where youth convenes, sport clothing is often donned to announce one's robustness. Frisbee-tossing males in cut-off football jerseys and gym shorts may actually enjoy the activity and the costume, but the significance of what's happening is deeper than that: animals in the wild often do mating dances to attract more passive partners, and male animals at the beach frequently do the same.*

Color or pattern coordination couldn't matter less, and the pieces should appear well worn, never new. Model: Cameron Hall.

NEAR LEFT. *Basketball jerseys are worn as casual tops for much the same reasons as cut-off football jerseys—to show off one's body and, by transference, to evoke the collective power of the team.*

When authentic pieces from a sport uniform are combined with non-specific sporty garments—sometimes called "spectator sportswear"—it is a mistake to go against the rugged athletic grain of the real pieces by trying for extremely spiffy fashion statements. Don't interfere with the trenchant sporty imagery by diffusing it. Model: Robert Henry.

137

of the physique. In addition to chest stripes to increase the apparent size of the torso, stripes that travel across the tops of shoulders or down arms and legs also make the body look bigger, more vigorous and thus more manly.

Many sports are played in shorts, so the male leg—banished from sight in the business world—is more visible in sport apparel than in other guises. The male neck is almost always in the open in sport clothing.

Sport clothing comes mainly in fabrics that stretch to facilitate movement. When wet with sweat, fabrics that stretch also cling to disclose more of the body. Even when dry, stretch fabrics conform to body movement. Since most sport clothing is not voluminous—excess fabric impedes good form by getting in action's way—and is pared down to few garments, body consciousness is augmented.

TEAM SPIRIT

Sports that necessitate very expensive equipment aren't imbued with the same physical appeal in their apparel as those which require less costly gear. Polo outfits, for instance, reek of rank and entitlement, since only the rich can afford to stable their horses and purchase all the esoteric paraphernalia. As a result, rather than conveying vigorous sportiness, polo and other equestrian gear doesn't ride well among most individuals.

Tennis is no longer an elitist sport, but racquets don't come cheap. (Neither do tennis lessons or court fees.) Thus, although tenniswear is widely worn as casual clothing, it still retains elements of snob-

BELOW FAR LEFT. Both rugby and soccer shirts have become so popular in recent years that even those with authentically wide chest stripes have assumed the aura of spectator sportswear and may be colored in atypical ways without losing a great deal of their athletic flavor.

In real competition, the shirts are usually worn with shorts. When adaptations are donned for casual off-duty purposes, other garments can be much more stylish.

Pleated pants in offbeat colors look especially good with innovatively colored rugby, soccer or, for that matter, tennis shirts. Model: Bob Martens.

BELOW NEAR LEFT. Most knitted shirts can be called into service for biking or even nonathletic casual occasions, but stretch-fabric biking shorts can't.

bism. And since tennis players aren't renowned for heroic physiques, tennis outfits aren't as sexy in their associations as some other athletic costuming.

Because it can be played on any open field with only one relatively inexpensive ball, soccer is a game for the masses, not the elite. Although the so-called lower classes have few privileges, they do enjoy a reputation for possessing more raw sexuality than the stodgy upper crust. (A derisive term for the rich is silk-stockings; think about it.) That the poor—whom the disdainful (and insensitive) wealthy lump together, claiming they breed like bunnies—can play soccer is one reason soccer clothing is sexier than gear for bigwigs.

Rugby falls into a similar category. Rugby stripes, often very bold and strongly colored, have become extremely popular in sporty clothing of all varieties.

Jogging outfits rank high in physical appeal because anyone can jog without huge expenditures.

Baseball gear isn't noted for sexuality because baseball is among the least continuously active of sports. Golf, which likewise does little to promote physical well-being, has unsensual connotations because it is played by the elderly, who according to myth lack sexuality, and because costly equipment is obligatory. Bowling does about as little for the body as golfing, and bowling gear doesn't earn high marks for sensuality either.

Activities related to aerobic activity—swimming, biking and running—are higher in sensual imagery, probably because these endeavors are truly healthful.

The dangerous sports—boxing, auto racing, skiing, surfing, hang gliding and sky diving—are also clothed in physical appeal due to the underlying link between adventure and sexuality.

A strongly contrasting striped shirt is a safety precaution because it increases the wearer's visibility. It does the same when biking isn't on the agenda. Model: Patrick Taylor.

BELOW NEAR RIGHT. Sailing gear is often very graphic and colorful, and jackets with nautical styling move well from the boat to the street. However, sailing outfits with matching jackets and shorts can look too specialized to make the same transition away from resort areas.

Sport tops combine more compatibly with nonsport bottoms than vice versa. Outfit: Catalina. Model: Terrence Dineen.

BELOW FAR RIGHT. Gear associated with water sports almost never translates into street fashion because of its extreme body-consciousness. Model: Jose Martinez.

RIGHT. *Authentic sport paraphernalia seldom crosses over into nonspecific usage. Here in the pool, the swim cap and goggles make sense because they are functional. Away from the pool they would be incongruous, since neither can appear to be other than what it is.*

By contrast, baseball caps are often worn for fun. Cap & goggles: Speedo. Model: Nelson Gonzalez.

INSET TOP. *The popularity of boxer swim trunks swells and ebbs, and then a new wave thrusts them into favor again. Pairs with flamboyant floral patterns are purposefully funky. Trunks (also inset lower right): Ermenegildo Zegna. Model: Cameron Hall.*

INSET LOWER LEFT. *The styling of swimming briefs changes little season to season because strong graphics and primary colors are always found in many of the designs. Briefs: Catalina. Model: Robert Henry.*

INSET LOWER RIGHT. *The bolder the stripes, the more attention they demand, implicitly telling onlookers to take note and to stand guard, since strong pattern suggests willfulness, sometimes even a desire to overpower. Model: Nelson Gonzalez.*

BELOW. Notice the date of the championships celebrated on this baseball jacket. The guy isn't old enough to have participated.

No, this jacket was bought in a thrift shop, and it is worn as a tribute to the national pastime and to wrestling as well (check out the figures on the badge) . . . and also to suggest that the fellow is in a rarefied league.

The authentically detailed jacket would look wrong with the outfit at left because the other's offbeat colors would be at odds with its "realness." The jacket would combine well with alternative "real" clothes—a plaid shirt and a pair of chinos, for instance—but not with "dress" garb.

ABOVE. When jogging became a mania, converts to the healthful activity flocked to buy jogging outfits.

Slowly at first, what started as a desire for fitness was transformed into a wish to look (not just to be) athletically fit, and designers turned jogging looks into fashion attire.

Sure, this fellow is running . . . in the same bright turquoise hooded sweat shirt and pale yellow knitted action pants he might wear on a date standing in line at the local cinema. Outfit: Ron Chereskin. Model (other photo this page as well): Nelson Gonzalez.

142

COACH CLASS

Active sportswear is deeper in physicality than spectator sportswear because the appearance of actual participation in a sport suggests greater prowess than that of a sports fan. However, even clothing designed with nonspecific sportiness emphasizes body parts in much the same way as the real stuff.

When you're wearing clothing actually created for athletic activity, bold color makes the authentic attire look even more authentic. Off-beat colors, especially emotional pastels, reduce authenticity. On the other hand, they can cut down on the inherent aggressiveness of sport attire without necessarily cutting back on sensuality.

Although sport attire is seen everywhere—jogging suits are as prevalent in the supermarket and at the public library as they are on jogging trails—this ubiquity does cut down on its expressiveness. Adopted by growing numbers as a substitute for other forms of off-duty garb, sporty attire may soon run the risk of becoming a clichéd look. This has already happened with jogging shoes. Sure, they're comfortable, and yes, they support the feet well. But they just don't go with any and every outfit. Jogging shoes look best with sportswear and jeans, less good with less conventional outfits and downright bad with dress clothes.

Beyond their comfort and support, jogging shoes have another advantage that can also be a detriment. Because they're almost always styled with contrasting pieces of material, often with white or another light color mixed with a dark or bright color, the interplay of pattern and color guarantees that someone will look at them. So jogging shoes are insurance that you'll receive a head-to-toe glance. That's just fine when all the pieces of your outfit fall well into place

SCORE CARD

Since sport apparel is naturally body-conscious, its shapes combine easily with each other in a natural way. The textures are smooth and durable to withstand wear and tear, so they too mix with a minimum of fuss. The primary and other pure colors prevalent in sporty garb, though hardly restful to the eye, seldom clash with each other, since it's only when dealing with atypical colors that coordination is problematical. Overall, the sporty mode is one of the simplest styles to conjure up.

In general, since sportswear was once functional attire to be worn while playing specific sports, the original details were seldom decorative; the integrity of the designs was first related to utility. When you wear sportswear as off-duty garb, some of the details are as useless as an appendix. Useless or not, they help the clothing retain its sense of genuineness. A football jersey without a numeral looks like a mistake. But to make a fashionable as well as a sporty impression, you must step beyond authentic sport clothing into the sphere of spectator sportswear, where imagination runs free without functional restraint. Although suede gym shorts make no functional sense when you're working out, they make fashionable sense when you want to project an aura of athleticism heightened by a sense of innovation. To some, fashionability is more invigorating than strict adherence to the rules of the game.

CHAPTER 7

SMART!

HIGHER LEARNING

We've all met the person who can memorize fact after fact about every subject under the sun but who still can't cross the street without getting lost. Primed with data galore and capable of discharging the scoop by rote, such an individual may have a high I.Q. but certainly lacks smarts. Having smarts means possessing the mental ability and agility to descend from the rarefied sphere of book learning into the mundane land of the living without stumbling on everyday paths. A smart person integrates knowledge from diverse disciplines and comes up with practical solutions beyond the books.

That smart is a word for quickness of thought and for sharpness of dress, as well as for deftness of wit and for shrewdness of insight, not to mention for rapidity of pace, is very much to the point when we're examining the style called Smart! The word smart covers a lot of territory, and so does this mode. Smart is never dull, but one can be smart in a number of ways.

Since smartness is expressed diversely, let's pinpoint how it differs from each of the other off-duty modes. As we review the styles from Sexy! through Sporty!, we'll remind ourselves of what makes the six of them tick. At the same time, we'll see how using smarts can transform all those looks in such ways that the results of the transformation can collectively be called Smart! Richly diverse, smartness has many guises.

BODY GILDING

To convey sexiness, the main emphasis is on body-conscious clothing. Garments are shaped to showcase the body and are colored to excite feeling. Onlookers are aroused by sexy textures and want to

LEFT. *Although clothing selection should always be thoughtful, "brain power" is more apparent in the Smart mode of dress than in the other off-duty styles.*

Details that onlookers might overlook aren't overlooked by the smart dresser. Underwear, for instance, might be smartly striped boxer shorts in chartreuse and pastel yellow. Model: Todd Neuhaus.

touch them. The appeal of the Sexy mode is entirely emotional, beneath thought and below the belt.

The Smart style, although it can contain sexy elements, has more brainpower than brawn. If clothing is shaped to showcase the body, then excitable colors are missing or are introduced only in small measure, and a commixture of tactile and smooth textures is likely.

Starting at the top, here is one example of a sexy outfit: in hot orange, a wide-shouldered shirt in textural linen, the top three buttons unfastened to expose the neck and a glimpse of the chest; in clear yellow, a fuzzy mohair cable-knit cardigan sweater vest, none of the buttons fastened; in brilliant rust, short-flyed, butt-clinging suede pants; lastly, tan grained-leather ankle-length slip-on boots with an elevated heel.

FAR LEFT. Although smartness is expressed in a variety of ways, unifying the different expressions is a thought-out originality of approach.

This outfit—akin to what used to be called a cabana set—is coolly colored in a sapphire blue-and-lime novelty print so eye-catching that initially the clothing takes precedence over the body beneath it. Onlookers are aware that thought has gone into concocting the outfit and that it is worn for purposeful effect. Thus, while body-conscious, the clothing also exhibits cerebration: it is Smart first and Sexy second. Outfit: Hector Herrera. Model (all three photos): Bryan Coolahan. Styling (middle photo as well): George Byron.

MIDDLE. Like the outfit just discussed, this one is also extremely attention-grabbing, but in a different way. The top is unlike most shirts, and the pants are hardly typical.

Once again, although flesh is revealed, at first it is of secondary importance, overshadowed by the magnitude of the clothing.

At first encounter, onlookers are immediately forced into deciding whether or not they find the outfit acceptable rather than responding only at gut level. This makes the ensemble's impression more "objective" than "emotional," even though reactions may be emotionally charged, since the outfit will not be overlooked and no one will abstain from judgment. Clothing: Artie & Cheech.

NEAR LEFT. The complex lineal design of this sweater optically broadens the chest and shoulders while framing the neck. If it were colored in advancing warm hues—perhaps in shades of brick red or tangerine—it would be outright sexy. But the colors—robin's-egg blue and cream—recede, dispersing some, though far from all, of the sexy appeal.

In exchange for the lessened sensuality, this coloration is thought-provokingly unusual. Sweater: G. Maislinger.

Leaving all the shapes and textures the same, let's recolor the outfit. Instead of the hot orange, make the linen shirt a cooler pale turquoise. Get rid of the warm, clear yellow by turning the sweater vest peacock blue. Cool down the suede pants with an ash gray hue. Exchange the tan of the boots for zinc gray. These transformations accomplished, the outfit can no longer be called truly sexy, even though every element—excepting the colors—is sexy. The color combinations are too offbeat to be seen as Easy!, don't mix enough moderation with all the colorful innovation to be perceived as Crisp!, don't include sufficient earth tones to come across as Earthy! And the shape of the clothing isn't Loose! or Sporty! No, this reassembled outfit exists in a place all its own: in Smart! territory.

It goes without saying that it's possible to rearrange the original sexy outfit differently. For instance, all the colors can be darkened. Then the hot orange of the shirt becomes burnt orange, the clear yellow of the sweater vest becomes mustard, the brilliant rust of the pants becomes an umber shade and the tan leather boots become walnut brown. This darkening process transforms the sexy ensemble into an Earthy! one, not one that's Smart!, because it isn't brainy enough: the color appeal is thoroughly emotional.

To transmute sexy outfits beyond sexiness into smartness, a shift in the color palette to include cool colors is necessary. If the palette is monochromatically based on one cool hue or analogously founded on two or more cool hues from related backgrounds, the effect is less emotional than when complementary colors are employed, since complementary combinations automatically have some warmth springing from their warm-cool contrast.

PACE BREAKER

To convey crispness through your attire, you juggle tradition, innovation and moderation in an upbeat manner. The cut of the garments is basically traditional and manly, the textures are mostly smooth and the color base rests in masculine hues chosen to be somewhat unusual in their own right while smaller doses of uncommon, more emotional color make fleeting appearances.

One aspect of smartness is to alter the crisp mix until crispness becomes so wholly upbeat that it transcends its genre. To see how that's done, let's take a look at a prototypical crisp outfit. We'll start with a knit polo shirt in pale blue. Over it is worn a Shetland wool V-neck sweater in an Argyle pattern, the diamonds in pastel yellow and hyacinth on a cream ground. The unpleated, straight-legged poplin trousers have pearl gray-and-white stripes. The Top-Sider shoes are navy blue with white rubber soles.

Crisp can become Smart through several means.

First, we'll do some recoloring. The polo shirt is no longer pale blue but carnation pink. The cream in the ground of the V-neck sweater yields to maize, and now the diamonds of the Argyle are orchid and ultramarine. The poplin pants are striped lilac and white. Color the Top-Siders plum with white soles.

The so-called masculine color base of the original outfit has been loosened, and sexually ambivalent hues—but not explicitly female ones—have taken hold. Yet all the garments are cut in traditionally manly ways, so their shapes exhibit no ambiguity. Convention is adrift in the newly colored ensemble, but the outfit is still moored in maleness . . . though the anchor is less weighted than before. On the other hand, the visibility of the wearer is greatly heightened by the new colorations, and this can be construed as an act of manly courage: only a very self-assured male dares to set himself up as a walking target for criticism by purposefully breaking time-honored color codes.

The first way to remodel crisp into smart, then, is to force more innovation into the color scheme by using large amounts of color not commonly associated with maleness.

Next, returning to the original outfit, let's change some of the colors and some of the textures. For the time being, we'll leave the shapes alone.

The pale blue polo shirt remains the same. The V-neck sweater is no longer a faintly fuzzy Shetland wool but a deeply textured hand-crocheted one with pastel yellow and hyacinth diamonds on a royal

BELOW. Wide-legged Bermuda shorts are a Smart hybrid of sexiness and crispness, with strains of earthiness and looseness, when they are colored a cool, frosty green. Other garments are needed to complete an outfit with a more definitive statement. Model: Les Lyden.

RIGHT. This cocoa-and-ecru houndstooth-patterned lap-over vest exemplifies the casual elegance that is often part of the Smart mode with Crisp overtones. It is striking enough that great support is unnecessary from the other garments.

For the outfit to be truly smart, additional colorful support is forthcoming anyway. The seersucker pants are pale cornflower blue and cream, and the knitted polo shirt is pewter gray.

This warm-cool color tension is typical of many Smart ensembles, Crisp or not. Outfit: Alan Flusser. Model: Patrick Taylor.

blue (not the original cream) ground. The pearl gray-and-white striped poplin pants are now maroon velvet with pale gray pin stripes. The Top-Siders are navy blue again. Soft and tactile fabrics now predominate over an outfit that initially was marked by mainly smooth ones. Yet compared with the second incarnation of the outfit, this tactilely textured one is colored in hues more drenched in traditional maleness. Its emotionalism stems now from texture, not color; but emotionalism isn't unchecked: the reserve of the royal blue and the steady regularity of the pin stripes counteract the emotionalism of the textures; it's a draw between emotionalism and objectivity.

Thus, a second way to remodel crisp into smart is to change the textures from mainly smooth to mainly tactile without disrupting the crisp color mix too radically and without changing the conventional shape of the garments.

Of course, if you choose, you can use both highly innovative color and strongly tactile textures in an outfit made up of conventionally shaped garments. That is the third way to recast crispness into smartness, and the result is more emotional than that of the previous example.

But let's not overlook the impact of shape.

Once again, let's return to the outfit as first conceived—pale blue polo shirt, Shetland wool V-neck sweater with pastel yellow and hyacinth diamonds on a cream ground and straight-legged, unpleated poplin pants striped in pearl gray and white. This time, though, we'll take the collar off the polo shirt so that it is left with a Henley neck— a rounded neck split in front by a reinforced stitched panel housing a few buttons. We'll also deepen the V of the sweater drastically, so that it stops an inch or two below the breastbone, and we'll broaden and lengthen the sweater while we're at it. What were once comfortably fitting pants are now almost skin-tight.

Newly shaped, the outfit has forfeited any claim to moderation or tradition in the cut of its garments, even though the colors remain only moderately innovative and the textures are mainly smooth.

As just seen, the fourth way to get smartness out of crispness is to reshape the garments untraditionally. No matter how traditional the colors or textures, clothing cannot convey crispness if the majority of the garments are cut unconventionally. Thus, when comparing the relative efficiency of shape versus texture versus color in shifting gears from crispness to smartness, unusual shapes make the move most swiftly and dramatically.

REST CURE

Of all the off-duty styles, the Easy mode is the least innovative. It takes inspiration to inject an impression of smartness into this placid mode.

The quintessential easy outfit is a conventionally shaped, comfortably fitting brown-and-green plaid flannel shirt under a camel-colored cardigan sweater, straight-legged tan corduroy pants worn with a plain brown leather belt and cordovan leather penny loafers.

Now, to change the coloration. Sticking with flannel, rid the plaid shirt of easygoing brown and green and brighten it up with a copper/ vermilion/chartreuse plaid. Color the cardigan more dramatically in lemon yellow. Keep the style of the corduroy pants intact but plunge in with emerald green. Allow the brown leather belt and the cordovan loafers to stay put.

Easy can become Smart only with color jolts to awaken it.

EXCAVATION WORK

Looking back to see how the easy outfit got its smarts, you might argue that the recolored ensemble belongs in the earthy mode and not the smart one. In truth, it does smack of earthiness, but the hues are brighter, more intense, than those naturally found in the earthy landscape. Still, more so than within the other off-duty modes, a great affinity exists between smartness and earthiness. After all, both represent an amalgam of several looks.

So how can Earthy become Smart? Perhaps the better question is: Why put the diverse earthy expressions through their paces to smarten them up?

Just to prove it can be done, we'll go to work on an ensemble laden with earthiness and citify its manner. For earthy openers, we'll begin with a tweed sport coat in a mixture of autumnal colors. Beneath it is a cable-knit turtleneck in forest green. The heathered flannel pants are a terra cotta shade. The Argyle socks are russet, chestnut and moss green, and the wing-tip shoes are burnt almond suede.

Even though the outfit looks great as it is, we'll eliminate the turtleneck sweater. In its place we'll introduce a pale cinnamon dress shirt with a contrasting white collar and a silk necktie in a geometric print of robin's-egg blue, sable brown, topaz and amethyst. The smooth textures of the dress shirt and silk tie aren't sopped with earthy connotations, but it's the visual brilliance shining from those last two jewel tones in the necktie that elevates the ensemble from mere earthiness into the more dazzling light of smartness.

As has been shown repeatedly, a change in color can transform any outfit strikingly. Of course, transposing shapes and textures from one style to another always alters the content.

LEFT. *Tweed sport coats almost always evoke countrified feelings, particularly plaid ones combined with flannel trousers and sweater vests.*

When colored innovatively, "country gentleman" outfits retain their Earthy ties but broaden their scope to incorporate an aspect that might be called the "city squire" look.

Here, some hues stray out of earthy country. In the sport coat, in addition to warm brown and beige tones, are found pale blue and pale yellow. And the plaid shirt contains pastel shades too numerous to mention.

Note the sweater's unusual neck; it's square, not the more customary V, adding to the Smart impression.

For whimsy, the necktie is woven with tiny skiers. Outfit: Alan Flusser. Model: Henry Mellen.

RIGHT. *This outfit is an amalgam of elements from several modes.*

Literally dozens of different-colored yarns, primarily in the green and brown families, have been woven to produce the highly tactile fabrics in the jacket and pants, so the color impression is rich and Earthy.

The proportions are all very roomy, and they recall the Loose style.

The way the shoulders are exaggerated suggests a form of body-consciousness found in the Sexy mode.

But the outfit doesn't come across as a hodgepodge. It appears original, a specimen unto itself, deserving the appellation Smart. Outfit: Jhane Barnes. Model: Benjamin Hobbins. Photographed in Venice, Italy.

EXPRESS LINE

The Loose mode is grounded in largely proportioned garments. Neutral colors, though not obligatory, are the standard choices. Knowing this, you probably think the way to transform looseness into smartness is by abandoning the neutral hues. You're right . . . for one of the ways.

To begin with, let's have a pair of emblematic loose trousers—contoured to the behind but long in the fly, with a waistband that

rests just atop the hipbones, the front pleated, the thighs full and the legs tapering to narrow cuffs—in linen, colored eggshell. A macramé string belt encircles the waist. The trousers are topped by a striated plaid linen shirt jacket of champagne, buff and iron gray. Beneath the shirt jacket is another shirt, also roomy, in ivory crepe de Chine. The hosiery beneath the smooth-leathered ash blond jazz shoes is smoke gray. Not bad, and very neutral indeed.

In addition to the neutral colors, this outfit also exhibits the smooth/soft textural mix typical of the loose style.

Keeping the same textures, we'll do a color switch. Turn the trousers cedar brown; the belt marigold; the striated plaid shirt jacket into solid jade green; the other shirt cardinal red; the hosiery raisin and the jazz shoes Bordeaux. Neutrality surrenders to the brilliant assault of advancing, intense hues. All of the colors are assertive, and strategically very smart in a skillful balance between warmth and

coolness, between subjectivity and objectivity. Stopping short of unruly flamboyance, this new look isn't for the meek, but its strength doesn't overpower.

It is also possible to transform the outfit as originally conceived—in total neutrality with smooth/soft textural contrast—by changing the textures either to all tactile or to all smooth ones without touching the colors. Either unpredictable step elevates looseness to smartness by making the outfit appear thoroughly conceived, carefully thought out, with a concentrated vision. When shapes are big and colors neutral, one expects to see textural contrast, so it's a sign of smartness to deliver the unexpected instead.

Another permutation. Although the assertively recolored outfit has smooth/soft textural contrast, the colors are very potent all by themselves—so potent, in fact, that they are significantly more important than the textures. If textural contrast is eliminated, the smartness

isn't undermined. With the same colors and the same loose shapes but with all smooth textures, the reassembled outfit will have great sleekness and will appear keenly cerebral. If the texture should all be tactile without alteration of the colors or shapes, then the outfit will be heartier, more emotional, Smart in a seemingly less premeditated way.

One other route remains to turn Loose into Smart: by making loose eclectic, by eliminating looseness from some of the garments and replacing them with non-loose but atypical ones. Eclecticism is always smart when it works. When it doesn't—well, it doesn't. You never know until you try. And since infinite are the ways to be eclectic in your garb, we won't even begin to compile a list. Experiment.

JOCK AND KEY

The Sporty mode, by relying almost completely on athletic imagery and pure color, is among the most artless of the off-duty modes. But sometimes guile is a sign of being Smart; so to instill smartness into sportiness, the style must become less categorical.

Color again, right? Right.

Here it is, a decidedly sporty outfit: a hooded sweat shirt in primary blue; a primary yellow tank top with a royal purple stripe around the chest; primary red gym shorts. Add white sweat socks with two red stripes circling the elasticized tops and a pair of pale blue-and-white jogging shoes.

Pick out any offbeat colors you like that coordinate smartly, put those colors on the garments of your choosing and you've made Sporty look Smart.

ABOVE LEFT. Would you prefer calling this a Loose outfit? You can if you choose, since tagging it Smart is fairly arbitrary. The colors are not mind-boggling; they're black, white and gray (except for the vintage Studebaker, which is yellow).

If it were not for the harness belt, the garb would indeed be called Loose.

But the belt is there, insisting on being noticed. In fact, so insistent is the belt that one ponders whether it has a special meaning, which in fact it has: it stimulates great interest, and that's why the entire outfit slips into a Smart slot.

By the way, that isn't a meaningless flap of fabric hanging on the shirt but an oversized pocket which, when in use, carries large items a smaller pocket couldn't. Outfit: Parachute. Model (exhaling cigarette smoke): Joe Dakota.

ABOVE RIGHT. Loose trench coat, loose sweater, loose pants—why isn't this outfit called a Loose one? Need you ask? Because the colors are exceedingly adventurous, of course. But since the photograph is in black-and-white, why tantalize you with a description? Take it on trust,

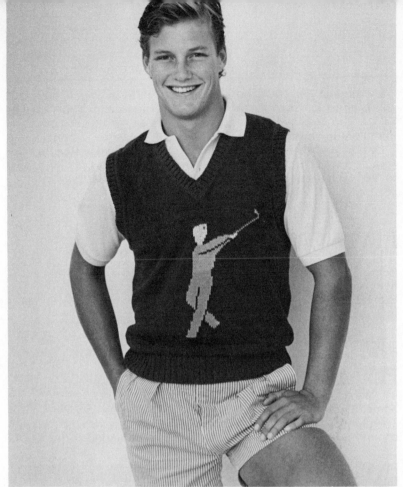

this is *Smart.* Sweater: G. Maislinger. Model: Bryan Coolahan. Styling: I Love Ricky.

UPPER RIGHT. If you have a favorite sport and want to let the world know, you may be able to locate a sweater with the appropriate graphics, and wearing one won't be a handicap when you want to add a *Smart* touch to *Sporty* dressing. Outfit: Alan Flusser. Model: Cameron Hall.

LOWER RIGHT. Even if you never made the varsity team, a spin-off of a varsity-style sweater will suggest that you did, and it has a decided advantage over wearing a relic from high school or college days: men who wear letter sweaters (and class or fraternity rings) from an earlier era often look to be stunted adolescents lacking in maturity.

A more mature fashion approach is to incorporate whimsy, not nostalgia, in your dress, and that is also a good way to give *Sporty* attire a competitive edge, transforming it into *Smart* apparel.

A graphic numeral could be the No. 1 choice in a cardigan sweater worn at play with gym shorts. Sweater: Robert Stock. Model: Robert Henry.

Of course, you could go eclectic here too—get rid of the gym shorts and add a pair of pants in the loose mode in an atypical color. Or you can employ juxtaposition; bring those gym shorts back . . . in red-orange leather.

By now you've got the knack. (And you've also just gotten through your review of the six other off-duty modes, so by now you know how to give each a smart expression should you so decide.)

REVEL CALL

Because someone with smarts integrates knowledge from many fields and discovers new truths that most others never think of, one expression of the smart mode is beyond description. Go for it. Revel in it.

POP ART

Something ironic happens whenever a fashion trend achieves mass acceptance. Whenever a form of dress is commonly seen, it becomes commonplace, and what is familiar is easy to overlook. The failure

LEFT. Some outfits are so spirited that they deserve to be called Smart. This is one.

The suit is principally in shades of black and gray, but the weave is very up-tempo. The background of the necktie is also gray, while the pattern contains a darker gray plus red and green. The shirt? Pink with thin dull red stripes.

Described in words, the ensemble doesn't sound all that exciting. But look at it. Jazzy! Clothing: Giorgio Armani. Model: Charlie Melite.

RIGHT. Formal occasions aren't all fun and games when it comes to wearing the right garb.

The philosophy behind wearing a dinner jacket is that attending males should be backgrounds to set off the finery of the females. For any man to claim too much of the spotlight is considered gauche.

How much is too much? Ah, there's the rub, and fine points can be—and are—argued. But few will argue that this shawl-collared dinner jacket is anything but Smart.

The pleated-front formal shirt is horizontally striped in red on white. The matching bow tie and pocket square are red silk with white dots. Outfit: Alan Flusser. Model: John Sommi. Hairstyling: Kent Rulon.

to "see" an outfit is the failure to read it. Conversely, when a mode of dress is rarely seen, this rarity ensures that an outfit will be seen and interpreted.

Clothing popularity has another drawback. Certain misguided people are so in Fashion's thrall that they are unable to see the individual for the clothes. In their eyes, there is only one way to dress: In Fashion. With their miswired antennae, they are deaf to all signals off Fashion's wavelength. Since most attempts to communicate with these people are doomed to failure, recognize that they're on a different frequency.

Even though trends and foibles cloud the issues, often you must pretend they don't.

FIRST MATE

A recurring theme throughout this book has been the disparity between dressing to suit yourself and quashing your instincts, dressing according to others' expectations. It's been said that if you can't please all of the people all of the time, at least you can please yourself. Realistically, you can't always do that either, not if you're mated or deeply involved. Like it or not, intimates inevitably attempt to influence our dress from time to time, if not regularly.

Generally, arguments over clothing arise when the person receiving the counsel suspects that the counselor is being arbitrarily willful or, worse, is being influenced by "the crowd." When we plan to wear particular clothing to a social gathering, for example, and someone close takes particular exception to that clothing, we feel that *we* are under direct assault, not just our clothing . . . and we bridle.

Whenever clothing becomes a potential source of irritation, think about the circumstances. To whom does the event have greater meaning, you or your mate (or date)? Which of you has more at stake? For instance, if you are attending your mate's class reunion, accept the fact that you will be an object of curiosity among those who were once your mate's classmates, not yours. It may mean little to you whether they consider you a prize catch, but your mate's self-esteem is on the line. (Idealistically, of course, it wouldn't be, but who can be philosophical about class reunions?) The event is comparatively far less meaningful to you, and you also have far less at stake. Defer. What's the big deal? You could argue that you will still be the same person whether you dress to your whim or to your mate's wish, but that argument can be reversed: deep down inside, you'll still be the same person if you defer and wear the garb your mate wishes. Don't mistake self-expression for obstinacy or mutiny.

But let's end the section on a positive note.

Many men are fearful of dressing adventurously, even though deep down they feel the itch to try, because they're anxious about being censured by Others. That's lily-livered.

Something happens when you start dressing freely. As long as you dress blandly, you are informing Others that blandness is the appropriate style for you. Your mode casts your mold. But as you become more adventurous in your garb, people begin to expect you to dress with free invention. In essence, they give you the license to be expressive once you start exercising that license yourself. That is true of off-duty and on-duty garb alike.

The only person holding you back is you. Let go and heave a contented sigh.

Now, smiling freely, onward to On-Duty Garb.

RIGHT. The odds are highly stacked against a reputable businessman's ever wearing a blushing pink suit during office hours. But what about during a vacation?

By juxtaposing the intrinsic seriousness of this traditionally cut suit with the emotionalism of the color pink, this outfit turns the tables on one precept of the Smart mode—namely, that nonemotional colors should generally predominate.

Ignoring color for the moment, this suit is earnest enough to pass as on-duty attire in any professional circumstance; it is steadfast to the core, clearly "objective."

But back to the color. In such large measure, it is so unabashedly the antithesis of earnest steadfastness that wearing it can only be interpreted as a deliberate put-on . . . and a tongue-in-cheek put-down of "serious" business, an inside joke.

Since humor, excepting the slapstick variety, is essentially more cerebral than emotional, the pink suit becomes Smart.

But the humor will be appreciated only in off-duty settings. It would be unwise to wear this outfit while applying for a loan. The loan officer might have the last laugh. Outfit: Jhane Barnes. Model: Lazaro Feleki. Photographed on the Greek island of Mykonos.

UPPER NEAR RIGHT. Top priority is seldom given to looking dashing while hunting, but adaptations of hunting clothes can look dashing, whether worn in the fields or on city sidewalks.

Here the garments are all conventional, but the color combination isn't. The shirt is printed with game birds. Among the least prevalent colors in the print are the blue-tinged-with-purple of the outdoorsy jacket and the emerald green-tinged-with-blue of the trousers.

Pairing these two colors is not standard, and that's one reason they look refreshing together. Another reason is that they are very harmonious.

A good way to come up with off-beat color combinations is to study the minor colors used in a decorative print and then to search for solid-colored garments in those minor colors to assemble with the printed piece.

Paying close attention to minor details is a Smart move. Outfit: Henry Grethel. Model: Michael Hart.

LOWER NEAR RIGHT. When several out-of-the-ordinary garments are worn in unison, the resulting outfit will inevitably look extraordinary.

Notice all the atypical detailing. The pants have tucked seams with no known function other than to create visual interest. Why the studs around the armholes of the distressed suede vest? No reason but decoration. And the contrast patches on the sleeves of the sweater are there for aesthetic, not practical, purposes. One scarf around the neck would surely do, but here there are two wound together for appearance' sake. Model: Blake Dawson. Photographed in the environs of Milan, Italy.

FAR RIGHT. Do you like the raised seams along this sweater? Do you agree that they add rugged textural interest? If not, there's a remedy: since the sweater is worn inside-out —deliberately, to expose those raised seams—they become quite ordinary when worn right-side-out. But not the sweater itself, with that dramatic slash of turquoise for an unexpected color punctuation.

The metal-and-leather belt is far from ordinary too. What's ordinary is never Smart, and what isn't, often is. Such as that beret. Sweater: G. Maislinger. Pants: Screaming Mimi's. Model: Neil Kramer.

OPPOSITE PAGE, UPPER LEFT. *Sexy or Smart? Check out the colors of the stripes: blue and white—nonsexy hues. By default, slap on the Smart label. Model: Patrick Taylor.*

OPPOSITE PAGE, UPPER MIDDLE. *Crisp or Smart? In Crisp outfits, the color base is composed principally of the so-called masculine hues, and highly emotional colors are limited in use. Although this sweater fits the description, the brilliant pink shorts don't. Incongruous with Crisp imagery, the outfit is unqualifiably Smart. Clothes: Alexander Julian. Model: Joe Dakota.*

OPPOSITE PAGE, UPPER RIGHT. *Easy or Smart? Easy outfits are so easy on the eyes that sometimes you can look right past them. These colors won't escape notice, although the clothing is fairly routine. To convey easiness, the hues would have to be blander. Left to their own excitement, these colors make this outfit a Smart one. Clothes: Cesarani. Model: Carter Collins.*

THIS PAGE, LEFT. *Earthy or Smart? These drawstring pants are myrtle green, an earth color, and the sweater has blocks of several hues, including mustard, another earthy tone, plus blue and yellow, which aren't. The shirt is white, a noncolor. Generally, texture is a secondary contributor to earthiness, with tactile textures conveying the trait. In borderline cases, when the colors—as in this instance—are insufficient to project earthiness unequivocally, texture becomes the determinant. Since the shirt and pants are both lustrously smooth, they are not on Earthy ground. By process of elimination this outfit receives Smart footing. Clothes (also far right): Ermenegildo Zegna. Model: Rich Olsen.*

THIS PAGE, MIDDLE. *Loose or Smart? Unquestionably the volume of these drawstring pants meet the Loose requirement—big proportions. But from out of nowhere (other than the designer's fertile imagination) there's an extra stripe woven darkly down one of the pant legs to make onlookers think twice. And the suede tank top isn't really large enough for Loose living. This outfit is ultrachic, deserving to be called Smart. Clothes: Andrew Fezza. Model: Tom Tripodi.*

THIS PAGE, RIGHT. *Sporty or Smart? True sportswear doesn't disguise its origins. Is this swimwear or jogging attire or weekend garb? The outfit has extras that don't belong to the authentic stuff. The jacket and shorts, for example, are both lined with bright yellow terry cloth. Functional? Perhaps, but wouldn't white terry cloth absorb the same amount of perspiration? The true purpose of the outfit is to make the wearer look good while maintaining a cool facade —not to perform well in the heat of the game. Tag this ensemble Smart. Model: Chris Brown.*

OPPOSITE PAGE BELOW. *Enough word games. Sometimes an outfit is so visually appealing that no conscious analysis is needed: one glance is enough to earn it the prized reputation for being Smart. This knitted shirt/sweater vest duo makes up such an outfit. Clothing: Alexander Julian. Model: Patrick Taylor.*

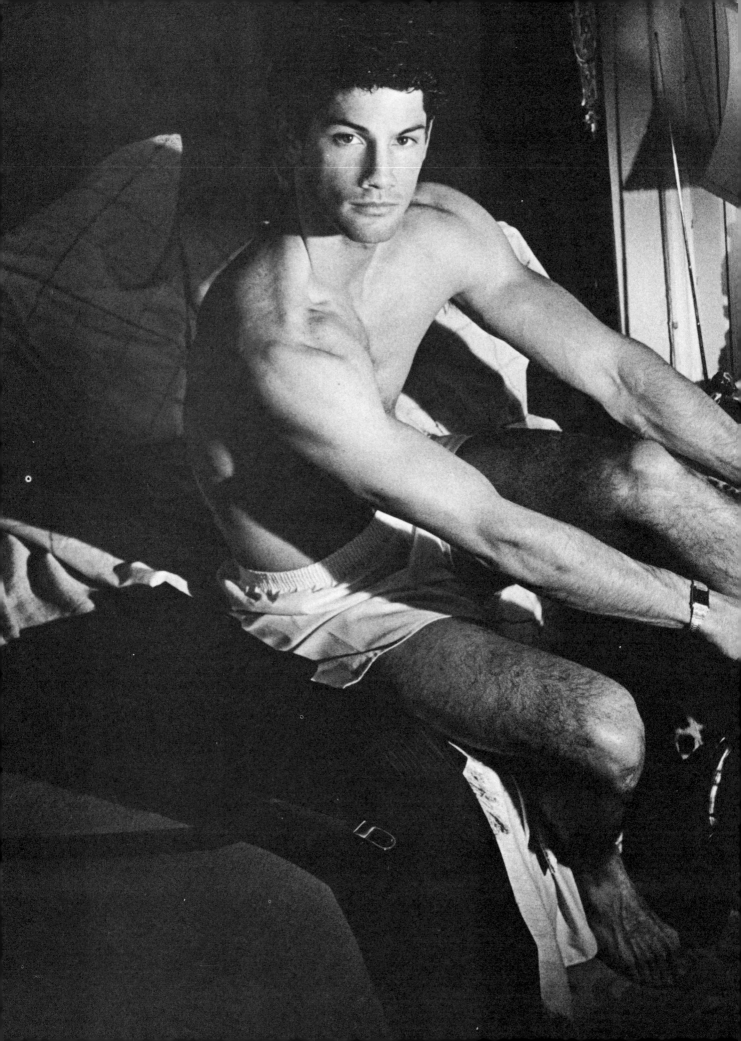

PART II
ON-DUTY GARB

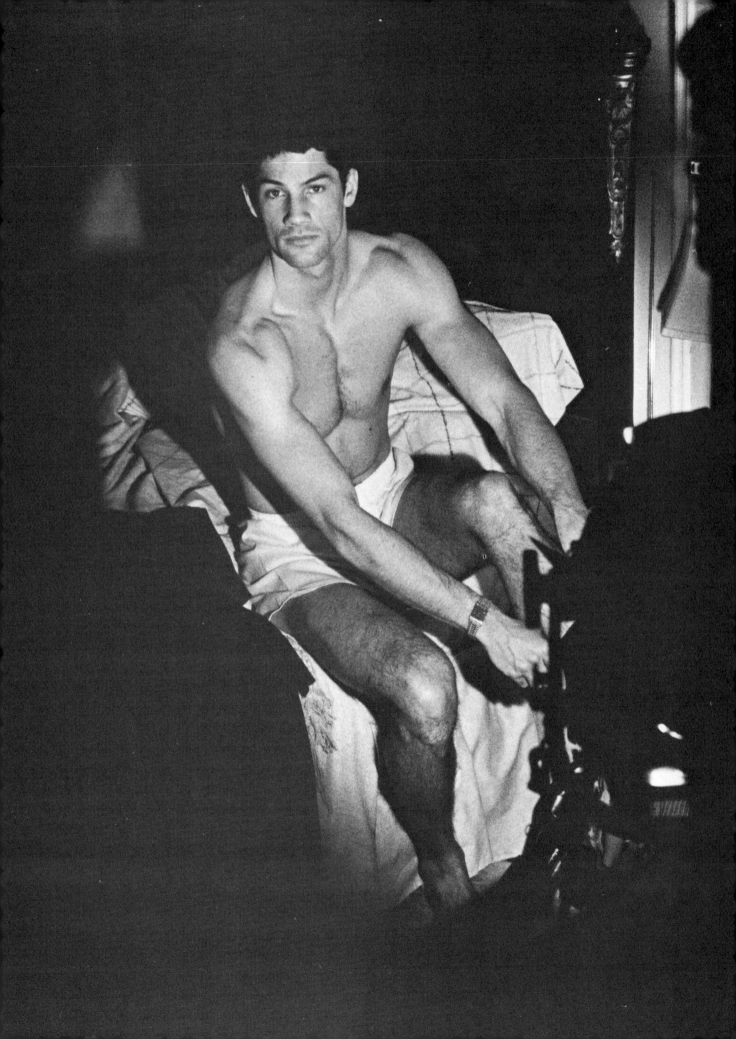

CHAPTER 8
RELIABLE!

SECURITY SYSTEM

Not every job entails wearing a suit and tie, of course; but in many occupations, if you don't make your on-duty appearances in dress attire you'll be at a disadvantage: there is a popular myth that a failure to dress "correctly" in professional settings signifies lack of interest in or knowledge of the job. Thus, a man who does not dress to the high expectations of others is not perceived as totally reliable. And being reliable is a very critical issue in the business world. In certain instances, you may wish to project something other than reliability, but it never makes any sense to suggest total unreliability. Thus, our exploration of the world of on-duty garb begins with a style called Reliable!

What does it mean to be reliable in business? A reliable person can be depended upon to get the job done with a minimum of fuss and fury. In truth, the work may not be completed with dazzling creativity or with mind-boggling rapidity, but come hell or high water, it damned sure will be done. Reliability equals steady dependability. Sometimes, a reliable person may also be a drudge . . . or may be perceived as such. On the other hand, sometimes it's better to be considered an earnest, steady worker who completes the job at hand than a temperamental genius who can't be counted on.

If some details on a suit jacket ever had any purpose in the past, their functions are forgotten now. Lapels today do absolutely nothing. Many of a suit's buttons are still there purely for meaningless show. Some pockets are sewn shut, never to carry anything. And what is more illogical than a necktie, a piece of cloth morbidly akin to a noose? (Some men insist that the necktie was devised as an instrument of torture.) Creased trousers are another affront to logic because they cannot be maintained except as an exercise in futility; since legs move and bend, human activity constantly battles the perfection of the crease.

PRECEDING DOUBLE-PAGE SPREAD. *Strictly speaking, on-duty garb is what someone wears to work, so a magician's cape could technically be called on-duty garb. Ditto for a sanitation worker's uniform and for the clothing of factory workers that could be identical in styling to what is normally considered off-duty attire. However, we commonly think of business clothing in terms of suits and ties, and there's even a style of men's hosiery that comes in an "executive length"—rising above the calf so that there's never the offending sight of the male leg in the professional sphere. Model (left as well): Pat Hardie.*

LEFT. *In the cold light of dawn before assembling his on-duty outfit, a man should consider his agenda when putting himself together, since different clothing combinations send out different messages. Reliable ensembles are much more somber than those which project "creativity."*

LEFT. In the business world, reliability is often demonstrated by conformity to clothing styles that really don't help get the job done. Wearing a suit and tie, for instance, will not increase an accountant's efficiency, yet many clients may think a casually attired accountant lacks "good sense" and will consequently distrust his professional acumen.

Similarly, certain details on business clothing help convey reliability even though they are totally without function.

Nonworking buttons along the cuff of a suit coat serve no practical purpose. Yet since such buttons are customary, to the conservative a coat without them seems to be missing something "essential" and is therefore "inadequate."

A close inspection of the cuff buttons here reveals that they are embossed with horse heads. A more conventional button style—bone buttons, for example—would convey greater reliability. Blazer: Country Britches. Model: Joe Dakota.

OPPOSITE PAGE. In on-duty situations, physical prowess should almost always be downplayed in favor of strength of character.

Shapeless, natural-shoulder suits do an exceptional job of concealing physical attributes, so they appear more reliable than shaped suit styles, and definitely more steadfast than a bare chest.

Although this suit is the height of reliability, the rounded shirt collar is not: with eyelets for a pin to hold the collar in place (and to show off the gleam of jewelry), the collar style is on the decorative side, which can be seen as a sign of undependable self-indulgence.

Though tasteful, the striped shirt and the striped tie are more adventurous than some fashion conservatives might like, and the outfit could be seen as slightly too innovative to be totally reliable.

Ironically, by committing a fashion error—the failure to leave a quarter-inch or so of shirt cuff visible beneath the sleeves of the suit coat—the man looks less dapper and therefore more reliable: high fashionability and a reliable impression don't mix. Suit: Hart Schaffner & Marx. Shirt: Henry Grethel. Tie: Francesco Smalto. Model: Todd Neuhaus.

What suits lack in practicality they more than make up in symbolism. By encasing their bodies in garments that are fundamentally illogical, men prove their willingness to subjugate themselves. The suit represents sacrifice. And this daily sacrifice—which is awfully close to penance—is thought to prove reliability.

Suits—some styles more than others—indicate reliability in another way. Unlike a lot of off-duty garb, suits are made with extra tailoring touches to create a shape that stays with the garment even when it isn't worn. The shoulders of suit coats are often padded, and the entire coat is usually lined. Extra pieces of fabric are engineered into the coat solely to impart dimensionality. As a result, the coat approximates the shape of a human torso . . . kind of. Since most suits are mass-produced, they are manufactured with an *abstract* male body in mind, not a particular man's own dimensions. Thus, when worn, the suit coat *replaces* the man's torso with the engineered shape of the coat. A man's physicality is lessened, since his actual anatomy is covered with an *abstraction* of a generalized physique. This new casing diminishes the uniqueness of the man's body and suggests that neither uniqueness nor physicality is desirable in this setting. So, to be reliable (the suit implies), you shouldn't appear unique, and your own physique—the evidence of your individual maleness—should be hidden. Conversely, if you expose too much of your uniqueness and your physicality, you will be suspected of being unreliable.

CLOSE RELATIONS

The reliable style is basically conservative and nonaggressive, but the degree of prescribed formality fluctuates from place to place. In many areas of the Sun Belt, for example, men's dress generally tends to be more informal than in the Northeast. However, in both regions, lawyers and bankers—members of professions in which formality is presumed—are expected to dress more formally than car salesmen. What constitutes the proper formality is all that changes. In the Sun Belt, a lawyer's or banker's needful formality may be attained with a tan gabardine suit; in the Northeast a pin-striped suit is deemed more befitting.

Just how freely you can dress when suits are on the agenda depends upon your job, your region, the crowd's expectations and your guts. High-fashion European suits are seldom worn on Wall Street, and Las Vegas entertainers seldom wear pin stripes. Who can gauge how their costuming affects their success? Still, the odds are high that lack of success can occasionally, if not often, be attributed to costuming. In dress and business situations, if you're not in a creative field, it's safer to veer toward the middle of the road. If you don't like playing it safe, don't. But expect to be judged more rapidly—perhaps negatively—than those who do.

Since the world of suits (or sport coats and dress slacks) and ties is less freewheeling than casual realms, you must pay close attention to details when donning on-duty garb. In the projection of reliability, details are particularly telling.

All the items in on-duty garb should relate to each other. The point of reference is usually the lapel width of a suit or sport coat. Arbitrarily, let's say the lapels are three and a half inches wide at their widest point (which is a fairly moderate width). For a tie to be correctly proportioned with those lapels, it too should be three and a half inches wide at its widest point. (You don't need to carry a ruler: just place the tie atop the lapel to see if the measurements are equal.) The length of the shirt collar likewise takes its cue from the width of the lapel. With a standard pointed or button-down collar, the length should be slightly less than the lapel width—in this case, about three inches.

LEFT. Despite his earnest expression, this fellow fails to convey all the reliability he would like.

No problem with the suit (excepting coat sleeves slightly too long, thereby concealing from sight a gentlemanly glimpse of shirt cuff). The shirt style and the width of the necktie are also acceptable for the reliable mode.

Not the pattern of either the shirt or the tie. The shirt's check is too graphic, and the wool tie is woven with tiny tennis-racquet designs.

Even with the businesslike attaché case, the outfit isn't essentially serious enough to be deemed strongly reliable when studied in detail.

Make the shirt solid white or pale blue, exchange the whimsical tie for one that's silk and solid or discreetly striped; then the outfit would truly suggest reliability. Suit: Hart Schaffner & Marx. Shirt: Henry Grethel. Tie: Rooster. Briefcase: U.S. Luggage. Model: David Spiewak.

Why is this so? Because with these proportions, the lapels, the tie and the shirt collar appear to be harmonious. If the shirt collar were very long—say, five inches—and the tie were very narrow—say, two inches—then the shirt collar would appear to be the most important element, since any comparatively larger volume increases relative importance. This remains true unless a relatively small item is colored so densely or vividly that the hue gives it disproportionate importance. In this example, the narrow tie, if colored neutrally, would be overpowered by both the shirt collar and the width of the lapels. No good. But it wouldn't be good if the narrow tie were colored brightly either; it would be a vivid exclamation point jarring in both its brightness and its narrowness. *All* elements should relate to each other without producing disharmony.

Lapel width also establishes the guidelines for the width of the pant legs. Any lapel above four inches across is considered wide; a lapel that measures less than three inches is said to be narrow; "moderate" lapels average out to be about three and a half inches wide.

When lapel width is moderate, pant legs should be only moderately wide, never of bell-bottom dimensions. Narrow lapel width? Narrow trousers. Wide with wide. When trouser legs are moderate, the waistband should be too. And if the pants are cuffed, the cuffs shouldn't be wide or narrow; moderate is again the correct dimension, about the same depth as the waistband. When trouser width is greater, the waistband and the cuffs correctly become wider too. Narrower, narrower.

Of course, there are some variations within these general guidelines, and remember that the guidelines are generalized for the reliable style. The most reliable suit comes in the American natural-shoulder mode with shoulder padding to "round off" the shoulder without extending it noticeably. The body of the coat hangs straight from the armholes to its skirt without any nip at the waist.

By contrast, sometimes suit and sport jackets are purposefully designed with waist suppression. Shaped coats are often accompanied by shaped trousers, proportionately wider in the thigh than at the knee and cuff.

When suit coats are cut close to the chest and hips, trousers tend to be narrow (and so do the lapels). When suit coats are cut wide in the shoulders and chest but narrow at the hips, trousers tend to be —but are not always—roomy in the thighs but narrow at the cuff (and the lapels may be any width, depending upon the design). In these two examples, the shifting proportions illustrate the designers' attempts to maintain balance and proportion. Far-out fashions often ignore these principles, which is why far-out looks remain on the fringe. Symmetry is almost always the goal in men's suiting.

In general, men's suits change only fractionally from season to season, so if the proportions of the ensemble are fairly close to correct (give or take a fraction or two), disaster won't strike. Only when combinations are openly belligerent or eccentric need you worry. During some periods wide lapels are popular, therefore fashionable. At other times narrow lapels are trendy. In the reliable style, being fashionable or trendy is not a primary goal. Moderation is.

SHAPE

Although most suit (and sport) coats have some engineered shape, some have much more than others. Compared with other styles, American natural-shoulder suits are more shapeless than shaped. This is their main asset in projecting reliability, since body consciousness is minimal, purposefully downplayed. Asexuality is the key,

ABOVE. *During business discussions, participants generally face each other, with the area surrounding their faces the primary visual focus. Thus, the proportions of garments near the face take on special importance.*

When the relationship between shirt collar, necktie and suit lapels is harmonious, you appear more "reasoned" than when the elements are disjointed.

Here is an example of perfectly balanced proportions in conventional business attire. The moderate width of the lapels is matched by the tie's moderate width, and the length of the collar points is somewhat less than the breadth of the lapels, as it should be, and also moderate.

These pleasing proportions are not dramatic in any way. This lack of visual drama is why the outfit suggests reliability.

By contrast, "fashionable" proportions are sometimes less harmonious and more exaggerated; they do not project reliability because they lack moderation. Sport coat: Austen Reed. Michael Hart.

173

which explains why women executives sometimes adopt variations for themselves on the reliable "manly" costuming of business suits. For both sexes, the style implicitly states that physical desire will never rear its head and mess up the works.

TEXTURE

Because sensuality has no place in the reliable imagery, neither do lush or luxurious fabrics. Workmanlike materials are prized. Tactility is eschewed.

COLOR

Since color so potently arouses passions, dispassionate colors are central to the reliable style. "Temperamental" colors containing "womanly" pinks or lavenders, reds or purples, are anathema. Re-

BOTH RIGHT. Reliable business attire never smacks of the sensual. There is a purposeful attempt to neutralize the physique by diverting attention away from it.

Here the tightly woven "hardness" of the poplin fabric erects a psychological barrier between the man's body and the outside world.

The conventional button-down-collar shirt, stiffly starched and spotlessly clean, symbolizes devotion to work, not play.

The strict regularity of the smooth tie also signifies close attention to detail.

The asexuality of this and other business looks is often adopted by female executives who also wear tailored jackets and neckwear to indicate earnestness. Suit: Country Britches. Tie: Jeffrey Banks. Model: Bryan Coolahan.

174

served colors in the blue family are preferred, but neutral shades are also good here.

In terms of pattern, mini checks and other small, regular prints imply reliability. Overscaled patterns that make grandiose statements are highly suspect. Restrictive tightness in pattern reinforces reliability. Round patterns are too suggestive of the voluptuary.

TIED UP

The necktie is the perfect symbol for the reliable mode because in all but the most isolated instances, it is obligatory. Yet it still must be a particular type of necktie—a smooth-surfaced, tightly woven, reservedly or neutrally colored one in a solid or restricted pattern. Knitted ties don't work, because their looseness could be interpreted as

BELOW. This muted plaid is a strongly reliable pattern, particularly when colored in neutral or blue shades.

The necktie's pattern isn't nearly as reliable. Despite its ordered geometric regularity, the motif is circular, and roundness is associated with womanliness, which in our society translates to unpredictability.

That's why this rounded shirt collar likewise fails to project a high level of reliability.

Although a double-breasted suit coat is not truly inconsistent with reliability, this one exhibits a great deal of flair; the overall impression is more of stylishness than of steadiness.

Notice that the lapels on double-breasted suits are wider than those on single-breasted ones, so necktie widths with double-breasted styles should be proportionately narrower. If they matched the lapel width, ties would look like bibs. Suit: Country Britches. Shirt: Jeffrey Banks. Tie: Francesco Smalto. Model: Todd Neuhaus.

laxity. A red tie raises the flag of disruptive emotion. Even a navy blue tie with pin dots, although a staple in classic menswear, doesn't quite pass inspection for absolute reliability. Pin-dotted neckwear is worn to "humanize"—that is, lessen the severity of—a business ensemble that might otherwise appear officious. On the other hand, polka dots —overgrown siblings of pin dots—are conclusively unreliable, because their roundness suggests the womanly. Larger coin dots bring clowns to mind. Except when diminished nearly to extinction, dots just don't seem dependable enough. No, the most reliable necktie is a medium blue silk one.

Other ties exist, of course, that are compatible with a reliable image. Diagonally striped silk ties in masculine hues, particularly those with narrowish stripes, look very orderly and self-controlled. Small geometric prints are also in this league. But highly decorative patterns like paisleys are too exaggerated to project reliability.

SUITS

As stated, the American natural-shoulder suit most satisfactorily meets the shape requirement for the reliable mode. A tan gabardine suit is fairly diligent in its appearance, but not as steadfast as a reserved blue one. Pin stripes are a small pattern with a strict regularity, so they are especially strong in projecting reliability. A neutral

gray pin-striped suit is a very good choice. The wearing of a vest also imparts reliability, since a vest adds one more clothing layer between the body and inquisitive eyes. Since a vest restricts body movement and is often unnecessarily warm in a centrally heated business environment, it also represents sacrifice of comfort to the rigors of duty.

Although a vested pin-striped suit is about as reliable as you can get, other suit patterns are not necessarily inconsistent with a reliable image. Very small checks in medium to dark colors, but never boldly contrasting light and dark, can also impart reliability—provided the accompanying shirt and necktie are not very high in innovation. Medium-scaled striped neckwear in subtle shades can coordinate with small-scaled checked suits for a reliable impression. But plaid neckwear cannot: that type of pattern mix is too adventurous for the fundamentally conservative reliable mode.

SPORT COATS

Sport coats can be reliable, provided they follow the rules of reliability. A navy blue blazer is fine, but a nubby tweed jacket isn't, because the latter is very tactile, too subjective. Generally, sport coats are less formal garb than suits. Their appropriateness depends upon the rank of the worker: the higher one advances in the corporate hierarchy, the less likely it is that a sport coat will meet clothing expectations.

LEFT. This outfit pushes reliability almost to its limit because it contains more stylish nuances than are generally associated with the mode.

Traditional but not pervasive, the mini check of the suit is not as reliable as pin stripes, but the pattern's tight scale is definitely consistent with reliability.

Not as consistent, but not truly at odds with the style, the tie is imaginatively figured with true stripes plus a geometric pattern, the suit pants are pleated, the pocket square has a paisley pattern inside its border for a small fillip of innovation and that's a gold collar pin holding the collar points in place.

None of these touches are standard in reliable dress, but none of them are inherently incompatible with it.

The vital question revolves around color. In neutral or receding colors, the ensemble manages, albeit barely, to maintain a reliable facade.

Should the outfit be colored in warm colors, it would become too advancing to be considered truly reliable. Outfit: D. Cenci. Model: David Spiewak.

RIGHT. Because this dress shirt is pure white, it can be thought of as reliable. In any other color, it would not be.

Look closely. The collar is on the short side—fashionably so.

What about the breast pocket? It is atypically "hidden," not the conventional "patch" sewn in place and exposed to the eye. And the fabric flap at the top of the secreted pocket is pleated at each side, another fashionable detail.

These are subtle touches generally absent in reliable garb.

Now take a look at the slacks. Those wide, deep pleats are also on the fashionable, not reliable, side.

The coarsely textured sport coat is much too tactile to impart stern reliability. Outfit: Jhane Barnes. Model: Benjamin Hobbins. Photographed in Milan, Italy.

DRESS PANTS

Pale trousers are not essentially serious, because their light tones imply an unreadiness to dig in. More earnest are medium and dark tones because they can conceal the figurative soil of arduous toil. Brown dress pants are very reliable in lower-ranked positions where the work is more likely to involve an element of physical as well as cerebral labor.

DRESS SHIRTS

A pure white, starched dress shirt is the height of reliability: if you play around in a starched white dress shirt, it will wrinkle and soil, giving you away. Finely striped shirts with white grounds are also reliable because of the regularity of the pattern and the purity of the ground. Some solid pastels are reliable—particularly pale blue and neutral beige—but pastel pink is too affectionate to be truly reliable: sentiment might supplant objectivity.

FOOTWEAR

Reliability includes a single-mindedness of purpose. Decorative details can be at odds with reliability because they can appear wantonly frivolous at worst, innocently beside the point at best. Because shoes are very revealing—they literally tell you where somebody stands—only straightforward shoe styles (such as "sensible oxfords") project reliability, and then only if they are made of smooth leather in brown or black or cordovan.

Socks should be equally sensible, either solid-colored or patterned on a small, tight scale. A reliable "rule of toe" is to match the color of the socks to the shoe color, or at least to approximate the same color value.

OUTERWEAR

A sensible overcoat is also the order of the reliable style. A trench coat with minimal detailing, because it is preeminently practical, is particularly good.

ACCESSORIES

Two accessories score high on the reliability chart. One is a wrist-watch with a leather (not metal) band, so reliable you always know the time. You won't waste it. When appropriate, a sturdy attaché case proves you will transport your work home without complaint. Flashy—or even understated—jewelry is unreliable, a self-indulgence. Belts are designed to keep your pants up, so why have a fancy belt buckle? Plain metal will do. Suspenders would be an affectation.

BLAND TIDINGS

As outlined above, the sum total of a totally reliable ensemble could be totally joyless. Without any alleviation in the garb, only reliability

LEFT. Although decorative shoes are generally inadvisable in the reliable mode, certain exceptions can be made. Take the matter of "cap-toe" shoes.

Often the cap is perforated with small holes—stylistic embellishments contrary to reliability. Here, however, there are no such perforations, only very subtle stitching across the cap.

Because the shoes are otherwise very "sensible," they are not fundamentally at odds with reliability, and they do inject a nuance of style which can be sorely lacking in extremely "sensible" outfits.

The tight-scaled pattern in the socks is likewise more interesting than a solid color.

RIGHT. This trench coat fails to convey the height of reliability because the decorative yoke, although authentic to the original style, is today an unnecessary embellishment.

Notice the way the belt is tied, ignoring the belt's true function in favor of a stylistic flourish.

If reliability were truly foremost in this man's mind, he would be wearing a less detailed, more androgynous style of raincoat.

But—and this is a big But—this particular coat, because it is drenched in tradition, is far more reliable than a fur-lined one would be, and in most situations it is unnecessary to project extreme reliability when a degree of it will do.

The coat is worn with a very reliable pin-striped suit, white button-down-collar shirt and understated striped silk tie. That the trench coat is somewhat more stylish than relatively more reliable styles doesn't make the overall effect unreliable, and this one concession to fashion over function augments the appeal of the whole. Coat: Gleneagles. Model: Patrick Taylor.

would be conveyed, with no sense of any other traits. Personality would be lacking. At times, this may be just what you want. In other cases, you might consider relieving the austerity of the style with a slight deviation here or there. For instance, simply pinning a discreet flower to your lapel could introduce enough spontaneity into the outfit to dispel unrelieved earnestness. Or, as another example, wearing offbeat Argyle socks could be a surprise tactic that isn't so overpoweringly surprising as to be shocking.

Another way to spruce up the reliable style a bit is to expend a little extra time in assembling the pieces and not to take the easiest way out. Simply donning a gray pin-striped suit with a white shirt and a medium blue silk tie is a very sure way to project reliability . . . very predictably.

Imagine this outfit instead: a navy blue suit pin-striped in a silvery gray; a pale blue shirt with a contrasting white collar; a silk necktie striped in shades of blue, silver and dark maroon; a maroon-and-silver checked silk square puffed in the breast pocket; a black leather belt with a small silver-and-gold buckle; black/navy/medium gray Argyle socks and highly polished lace-up cordovan leather shoes. The pieces are mostly reliable, the overall effect is definitely reliable, but a touch of style is also present, as is the sense of a distinctive, somewhat distinguished personality. Here, there is reliability *plus* sureness and controlled originality. The first outfit was bland in its moderation; this one pleases the eye by moving moderately beyond blandness.

LEFT. To some, the matching striped necktie and pocket square here will represent the epitome of class and dash. To others, the effect will look much too calculated. So what else is new?

Although it takes greater innovation and imagination to successfully mate a tie and pocket square with nonmatching patterns, particularly when both the suit and shirt are also patterned, strong innovation can be at odds with projecting a reliable aura.

Given the other components in this ensemble, if the pocket square were a check or paisley print, reliability would be diminished.

If the body of the shirt were solid and not striped, however, thereby eliminating one pattern from the outfit, then replacing the matching striped square with a check or paisley one wouldn't alter the degree of reliability conveyed.

The elimination of the pocket square entirely would increase the impression of reliability . . . at the expense of stylishness and personal expression.

As presented, the outfit is reliable and *stylish* without pushing too hard or too far.

Dressing—like life—isn't always simple when you're faced with choice. But freedom of choice has its compensations: you are in the driver's seat determining your own destination. Suit: John Weitz for Palm Beach. Model: Pat Hardie.

CHAPTER 9

SINCERE!

HEART FELT

You can't force yourself to be sincere in the same way you can oblige yourself to act reliably. Reliability involves a conscious decision to exert willpower and stems from a sense of obligation, but sincerity is a matter of sentiment, a subjective rather than an objective trait. Reliability is equated with dispassionate discipline; sincerity is equated with compassionate understanding. Reliability originates in the mind. Sincerity comes from the heart.

For many, the on-duty world of business is the battleground for ruthless competition. Getting ahead is all. In the relentless rush to reach the top, if someone else's toes get stepped on—or someone else's back gets the knife—well, that's inevitable, isn't it? The person who doesn't look out for Number One doesn't know the first rule of professional advancement: nice guys never finish first.

Some rare individuals would rather stay put at a lower rung on the corporate ladder than forfeit their status as nice guys. Mindful of the feelings of others, particularly of subordinates whom they steadfastly refuse to debase through power plays, these compassionate fellows believe that any business enterprise is a people business, not that people exist only as replaceable parts in the business machine. Perhaps they're idealists, hopelessly naive, but no one will ever convince these men that the bottom line is profit. For them, the only aim worth pursuing is decency.

Does sincerity rank high as an attribute in the business world? Possibly not. However, it has singular ranking for the men and women whose self-respect hinges on playing it straight, doing the right thing according to their own ethics and, corny as it may sound, their own sense of humanity: for them, to be careless of others' feelings is morally wrong, unjust. With empathy to spare, they believe that any harsh deed they commit is an open invitation for others to treat them in the same callous way. They likewise recognize that any

LEFT. Sincerity is an emotional trait expressed in feelings more than facts and figures. Sincere clothing is also more subjective than objective. Pants & suspenders: Alan Flusser. Dog: Yoko. Model: Kevin Gouchee.

Sincerity in dress is often transmitted on a subliminal level. Without close analysis, it's easy to see that both these outfits appear "friendly."

Here's why: the shape of every garment is traditional and classic, so no demands are placed on you to decide whether you like them or not; without thinking about it, you "accept" their presence.

The houndstooth pattern of the sport coat at the left is likewise a traditional classic in menswear, so it offers nothing challenging. The pale-colored V-neck sweater is warming.

On the right, the casualness of the corduroy suit is tactilely inviting, while the Argyle pattern on the sweater is a familiar design motif in menswear and therefore is easily "understood" without thought for hidden meanings or motives.

Colored in warm tones, both ensembles emanate sincerity in a way that garments more aggressively fashionable do not. Outfits: D. Cenci. Models (left, right): Ron LaRussa, Neil Kramer.

The loose weave of this cowl-neck sweater is so tactilely pronounced that its "softness" is aggression-free. The necktie is likewise very textural, signifying easy approachability.

Meanwhile, the conventional striped dress shirt roots the outfit in manliness, and the medium-dark tone-on-tone plaid of the sport coat injects some reliability, so the impression isn't overly soft.

The darkish tones in the plaid coordinate well with the hues of the necktie. If the sport coat were a lighter shade, the necktie should also be paler. Otherwise, as the only dark element, the tie would stand out too much and call extra attention to itself for no good reason. Outfit: Richard Gaines. Model: Charlie Melite.

act of prejudice is an assault on every human being, since only through the accident of birth are we not someone else. Cutthroat business tactics are simply beyond these people's ken. They have too much heart.

That sincerity is a heartfelt emotion is the key to the style called Sincere! Paradoxically, in many ways this new mode is the antithesis of the reliable style but nonetheless owes it a sizable debt. The shape of sincere garments tends to be fairly commonplace (as in the reliable mode), but the textures and colors associated with sincerity are greatly at odds with those conveying reliability.

SHAPE

On-duty garb is not noted for breathtaking diversity in its styling, and a man wearing unconventionally shaped attire will always appear to have made a purposeful decision to dress in an unusual way. Although originality and sincerity are not mutually exclusive, great originality implies a deliberate assertiveness that can be overpowering. Combining unorthodox textures and colors with an atypically shaped suit produces a look too self-consciously willful to convey the gentle subjective quality of sincerity. But traditional garments are strongly masculine and require softening to project sincerity.

TEXTURE

As you know, "emotional" textures have tactile surfaces. Since sincerity is an emotional trait, tactile textures help convey this characteristic.

COLOR

Emotional colors are also employed to project sincerity, but carefully, because on-duty garb must always manifest a measure of reliability. Without some purposeful seriousness, the attire could be mistaken for off-duty garb. Since extreme emotionalism can suggest instability and is therefore undesirable in the business milieu, heavy doses of emotional colors are inadvisable. Neutral colors, mixed with warm and advancing emotional colors, should predominate to stabilize sincere on-duty garb. Consequently, the emotional hues occur principally in shirts and neckties, while suits, sport coats and dress slacks are mainly neutral with only minor infusions of emotional shades.

In patterns, plaids are less formidable than stripes, so they are useful in projecting sincerity.

SPARE PARTS

Since most suits are more formal than most sport-coat-based ensembles, sincere on-duty garb often incorporates sport coats, although some suits—particularly corduroy and tweed ones—fall easily into the sincere classification. Sweaters and sweater vests also have secure places in the sincere style because they are adroit at adding soft textures and soft colors without minimizing the serious integrity of other clothing pieces.

SUITS

A tan suit is more sincere than a gray one because the hue tan contains a hint of yellow, a warm color, whereas gray is more distant. Similarly, a brown suit is more sincere than a blue one, because

earthy brown is more emotional than reserved blue. In general, earthy neutrals—tans, beiges, olives, khakis, browns—convey more sentiment than dispassionate grays. But several yarns of different hues are often mixed together to achieve what is apparently one solid color, so even gray tones are not all alike. By studying fabrics in strong light, you can often discover yarn colors not immediately visible at first glance. This will help you distinguish the differing underlying personalities among seemingly similar hues, because we all are influenced by colors' "hidden meanings." Although we may fail to register these subtle distinctions consciously, subconsciously we "see" them. We respond to "invisible" color codes because they're not truly invisible, just difficult to sort out by eye. Also, some fabrics are "heathered"—woven to have a rather mottled appearance, so you can't figure out what exact colors they are. Heathered tones are generally soft, and the "blur" of the mix reduces authority, thereby imparting some subjectivity.

A heathered tannish flannel suit, a brown herringbone tweed suit, a cream-and-chocolate brown checked suit—all of these share a basic sincerity while still maintaining enough neutrality to satisfy business demands . . . provided an impression of strict authority isn't required. To achieve a sincere look, you must sacrifice power imagery. On the other hand, a suit can't impart any trait all by itself. Other ingredients affect a suit's basic message.

SPORT COATS

Sometimes patterns can take the place of textural tactility. Plaids appear to have depth even on smooth, flat surfaces, so a plaid sport coat needn't be of a nubby or tweedy fabric to project sincerity. Yet for a look that's especially sincere, nubby or tweedy fabrics do help. To compound sincerity even further, introduce a pastel or warm color into the nubby or tweedy plaid. Although stripes are more authoritative than plaids, tweedy striped jackets convey sincerity when properly colored in earthy neutrals and warm or pastel hues. Inserting a square in the breast pocket softens the strict manliness of a traditional sport coat and adds to a sincere impression.

DRESS PANTS

Trousers must coordinate with sport coats (and other garments too), so a range of styles may or may not work. Although mixing several pronounced textures and patterns has become increasingly widespread in men's clothing lately, doing so goes beyond the parameters of the sincere style, because this technique is too adventurous to be entirely trustworthy. In many people's eyes, being extremely "fashionable" means being self-centered, so wrapped up in oneself that no room is left for the concerns of others. Thus, great fashionability is at odds with projecting sincerity. For this reason, conventional straight-legged dress pants tend to be the safest bet. Heathered flannel is a good fabric choice, as opposed to smooth and flat-surfaced serge and gabardine, which are too hard to be seen as sincere. When more casual trousers are allowable, corduroys do nicely. However, if the sport coat isn't highly nubby or tweedy—say it is a camel-colored cashmere blazer—then tweedy or nubby dress slacks are very welcome. Medium-toned or pale colorations project more sincerity than darkly austere shades.

DRESS SHIRTS

The dressier the shirt, the more firmly it announces that hard-nosed business is being conducted. Casually styled shirts worn with neckties are less unyielding, so they speak more eloquently of the human

BELOW LEFT. The V-notch of this sport coat is higher than that of the cashmere jacket. So is the button closure. These traditional details increase this one's conventionality.

However, the pale tan color and the visibly textural weave are not authoritative, nor is the plaid shirt, which could easily be worn as a casual, off-duty shirt.

The knitted tie is similarly low in power imagery. These softening details increase the impression of sincerity. *Clothing: Cesarani. Model: Ron LaRussa.*

BELOW RIGHT. This outfit is too unconventional to be perceived as sincere, even though all the elements (excepting the bow tie) could individually be considered sincere. The difficulty—which is problematical only when the goal is to convey sincerity—is the use of profuse pattern, a ploy too innovative (though tasteful and well executed) to pass one important test of sincerity—that an outfit should appear fundamentally more conventional than adventurous. *Outfit: Cesarani. Model: Chris Grey.*

factor. Since plaids are widely used in off-duty garb, plaid dress shirts start out their business life with casual associations and convey sincerity. But if they're worn with a plaid sport coat, they don't; they convey confusion *unless* the plaids are skillfully and tastefully combined, which is no mean feat. Usually the only way two plaids coordinate is when both are in very similar colorations, with one of the plaids in a small scale while the other is largely scaled. Even with perfect execution, mixing plaids connotes a sartorial finesse more reminiscent of the Ingenious! mode (Chapter 10) than of sincerity.

Stripes combine more easily—and sincerely—with plaids *if* the stripes aren't too authoritative (pastel hues cut down on authority, remember) and if the scales of the two patterns aren't combative. Very pronounced plaids and very emphatic stripes fight like the devil. The muted plaids of tweedy sport coats are much friendlier with distinctive stripes.

Perhaps the most sincere dress shirt around is the pink oxford-cloth button-down-collar model. On close inspection, oxford cloth isn't as smoothly flat as finely combed cotton fabrics. It has a slight texture, and that's desirable when conveying sincerity is your goal. Pink is a very friendly, pacific color. Combine oxford cloth and pink, and you've got sincerity. Optimistic yellow is another extremely sincere color.

NECKTIES

Knit neckties have more tactility and textural interest than silk ones, so they impart greater sincerity, especially when they're colored warmly. Ditto for woven wool ties. Medium-scaled patterns are more

sincere than tightly restricted ones on any type of necktie, silk included. However, large-scaled patterns are not sincere because they suggest self-interest above concern for others.

SWEATERS

Most sweaters are very tactile and thus exhibit an intrinsic emotionalism, so they usually appear sincere. In recent years, one sweater style has been promoted as a vest substitute in business attire by so many designers that it often seems a hallmark of the sincere mode. This sweater style is the Fair Isle, woven with colorful geometric patterns in an array of colors. Although Fair Isle sweaters come in long-sleeved crew-necks and V-necks, most commonly they're seen as sweater vests, and that gives them extra applicability as on-duty garb: they fit more comfortably beneath suit and sport coats than long-sleeved sweaters do. They are fairly easy to coordinate with other patterns and fabrics, particularly tweeds, with which Fair Isles are almost always naturally compatible. Also, when styled as a vest, the Fair Isle allows clear visibility of the shirt and necktie worn beneath it.

The deep-rooted sincerity of Fair Isle sweaters doesn't mean that other sweaters can't impart sincerity, of course. Almost all do. Fair Isles just do the job easily and well, without a lot of effort. But even they won't make a go with strongly patterned plaids. Solids aren't the only alternative with plaids, however. Imagine a big cross drawn on the front of a sweater, dividing it into four parts. Now imagine that those four parts are all of different colors, so that there are four color blocks. Unless the scale of the plaid sport coat is extravagantly large, a color-blocked sweater can be paired handsomely with it as long as all the colors are simpatico.

FOOTWEAR

Shoes are more indicative of personality traits than many people realize. Suede shoes, for example, have more tactility than smooth leathers and thus are the friendlier of the two. Shoes trimmed with perforations and stitchings—as seen on the classic wing-tip brogue,

ABOVE. Sweater vests add tactile qualities that give heart to business outfits. Colorful geometric Fair Isle sweaters like this one work especially well with nubby tweeds.

Although knitted ties are generally more emotional than silk ones, sometimes the design of a smooth silk tie imparts sincerity too. Here, the repeating motif of Scotties conveys puppyish spirit.

Neckties with pictorial representations like this fall into the category of "club" ties, even though they may never have been adopted by any known club. Outfit: Jeffrey Banks. Model: Chris Grey.

LEFT. Because of their brushed texture and the decorative detailing on the toe, suede wing-tips are a good choice of shoe style to convey sincerity.

Here, taking the place of more customary solid-colored socks are ones with intersecting lines to create squares.

The socks "bridge" the colors in the tweed pants and the shoes because the value of their hue is midway between those two.

RIGHT. Classically styled polo coats are always considered proper businesswear, and they have the extra advantage of conveying warmth as well as providing it. Camel is an excellent color choice to project sincerity.

A pale-colored plaid scarf likewise does the job better than a stern, dark scarf would.

In hats, paler tones are preferable to very dark hues that are high in authority. However, light-colored headwear, particularly during the winter months, is often considered unbusinesslike. Thus, a medium-colored felt hat is a good compromise between reliability and sincerity.

For on-duty purposes, the hat brim should always be turned down, because upturned brims are seen as either sporty or comedic, never serious.

The crown of the hat should not be too tall if you don't want to suggest that you have a head swollen with self-importance.

Center creases on the crown are considered gentlemanly. Topcoat: Hart Schaffner & Marx. Hat: Screaming Mimi's. Tie: Cacharel. Model: Michael Principe.

with "winged" medallions on the toes—exude more sentiment than no-nonsense plain-toed oxford lace-ups. Rust-colored suede wing-tips project a high degree of sincerity. In smooth-leathered shoes, a sincere style is the cap-toe type, with an additional outer covering at the tip of the shoe, usually applied straight across, with perforations along the straight line.

Hosiery also has a fair amount to say. Black, dark blue and brown socks speak of strict conventionality. Socks in offbeat colors whisper subjectively when the hues are subdued and shout temperamentally when the hues are vivid. Bright red socks aren't sincerely emotional because they're clamorous. Pale rust socks are sincerely emotional because they're soft-spoken enough to appear caring, not aggressive.

Generally, shoes and socks should be considered a harmonious duo and should be in similar tonalities. If the shoes are dark, then dark hosiery is usually preferred. If the shoes are pale, pale socks are advisable. Mid-tones go with mid-tones.

Although some contrast is allowable and inevitable, in the realm of on-duty garb shoes and socks should not be in a vastly different tonality range from the accompanying suit or dress pants. Since pale and medium-toned colors are more affectionate than earnest dark ones, it makes the most sense to stick to mid-toned footwear, which can be worn successfully with either pale or medium-toned trousers,

and even with dark ones should they be part of a sincere ensemble. In fact, medium-toned footwear alleviates some of the earnestness of dark trousers. In this latter instance, hosiery should "bridge" the shoes and trousers—be paler than the trousers but darker than the shoes.

OUTERWEAR

Camel's hair—the real luxurious thing or an imitation—has a nap to it that implies warmth, both for the body and for the nature of the wearer. It is likewise a warm color. So it's not surprising that a camel's-hair polo overcoat—a rather loosely fitting garment with a full belt or a half-belt across the back, usually with large flapped pockets—is tops in the sincere mode.

ACCESSORIES

Gold is a warmer metal than silver, so gold projects more sincerity than silver. But chunky jewelry isn't sincere; it's ostentatious. Since the sincere style is rich in textures, it requires little assistance from accessories to make itself felt.

FAIR PLAY

Thus far we've discussed on-duty garb only in terms of suits and dress attire. Obviously, many people work in positions that don't call

BOTH ABOVE. These two outfits are in decidedly different moods, but the same pants—a tan "cut corduroy" pair with the raised cord sheared for lush tactility—appear in both, proving that some garments can make the transition from off-duty to on-duty garb.

Of course, pieces from the sincere wardrobe, because of their relative informality, shift gears more readily than garments that are more hard-nosed in their business connotations.

Should someone attempt to combine pin-striped suit pants with a sweater jacket, for example, few on-lookers would fail to notice that the pants are actually only on loan from a suit.

Here, by comparison, the pants appear integral to both the dressed-up and the dressed-down versions. Pants & sweater jacket: Ermenegildo Zegna. Sport coat & tie: D. Cenci. Model: Carter Collins.

BOTH BELOW. Like the photos on the opposite page, here are two more outfits in divergent moods even though one of the garments—the rust-and-brown tweed sport coat—appears in both.

The ensemble with the twill-and-corduroy jodhpurs is in the earthy "country gentleman" spirit.

The ensemble with the tie would also be called Earthy if worn in an off-duty setting. For on-duty purposes, the effect is Sincere.

In general, tweed sport coats are highly adaptable. But jodhpur pants aren't: it's inconceivable that they would ever form part of a business look. Both outfits: Robert Stock. Model: Pat Hardie.

for such rigid dress. Some fields—advertising and publishing among them—allow great flexibility. An employee may wear dress attire one day and casual garb the next. If you are in such a flexible professional situation, modify the guidelines given here. For instance, you can undoubtedly see some similarities between the Sincere! on-duty style and the Easy! off-duty mode. They both rely on tactility to eliminate aggressiveness. And they both employ emotional colors, although comparatively more of them are found in the sincere wardrobe. Thus, if you're adapting easy off-duty garb to make a sincere on-duty impression, simply color some of the easy garments more warmly. For example, in off-duty contexts, corduroy pants are worn with a flannel shirt to convey easy friendliness. The same corduroy slacks can also be worn with a tweed sport coat to project sincerity in an on-duty milieu. If those slacks are a warm bronze color, they will appear more sincere (subjective) than a similar pair colored steel blue (objective).

Reversing the off-duty/on-duty order, the same sandy brown tweed sport coat worn with charcoal brown slacks to convey sincerity in the on-duty sphere can be paired with chino pants and a checked sport shirt to appear moderately dressy in an easy off-duty context.

Most clothing other than suit coats freely crosses borders when you put your mind to it. You should always look for ways to mesh apparel from the two spheres. That increases the flexibility of your clothing by having it perform double duty. When you expend some imagination, you'll be pleased to see how often play clothes can become work clothes, and vice versa. While individual garments carry their own associations, those associations are altered when the pieces join other pieces in new combinations. Nothing is as constant as change. Keep changing and enjoy the free flow.

CHAPTER 10
INGENIOUS!

DIFFERENT STROKES

A person can be reliable and sincere . . . and a boob.

A person can be clever, insightful, bold and brilliant, but not at all reliable or sincere.

If you were to hire an employee, which of these traits would you rank most highly: reliability, sincerity or ingeniousness? It would depend upon the position you're filling, wouldn't it?

The shortcoming of most dress-to-succeed manuals is their failure to come to grips with the unalterable fact that not every job is like every other one, and the undeniable fact that not every man is like every other man. For instance, you often hear the old saw that the way to get a job is to dress like the person who's doing the hiring. If you're looking for a job in the personnel department and you're being interviewed by the personnel manager, the tactic might be productive. But if the opening is in the art department, the ploy could flop. Also, sometimes job interviews are held for nonexistent jobs, simply so that the interviewer can become acquainted with a prospective employee. In this instance, it's impossible to outfit yourself according to another widespread maxim—to get a job, dress as if you already occupied it—since you have no conception of the position for which you might eventually be evaluated. Should you dress extremely conservatively for the interview (another piece of standard advice), the interviewer would probably consider you only for upcoming openings in which conservatism is deemed desirable. And you could miss out on a job in which unbridled imagination is the top priority.

Although it sounds iconoclastic, consider the logic of dressing for a job interview to showcase your own personality and your strongest traits. When you do so, you present yourself honestly, with no attempt at deception. Although you will be passed by for some jobs,

LEFT. *The ingenious style comprises innovative attire that may not always be immediately identifiable as on-duty garb. Since the necktie is the symbol for the entire professional wardrobe, unusual neckwear—or none at all—may be one pertinent element in projecting ingeniousness. Model: Todd Neuhaus.*

LEFT. You can make an ingenious impression in a number of ways, although the central strategy is always to catch observers unprepared for your clothing combinations.

Here the components are not unique, but the way these components are put together is imaginatively original. The individual patterns are all kinetic; in concert, they exude highly charged energy.

First consider the herringbone pattern of the sport coat. Alive with movement, the same "give-and-take" weave is found, in smaller scale, on the striped necktie, where the broad dark stripes provide a rest from all the activity.

The very small-scaled checked dress shirt almost appears to be one solid color, except there is greater dimensional movement here than in a nonpatterned fabric.

Why does this combination look handsomely ingenious instead of eccentric? Because of the progressive scale of the patterns.

The shirt starts the activity on a small, tight scale. Next comes the medium scale of the herringbone coat, clearly noticeable but not overwhelming. The largest pattern is found in the wide stripes of the tie, but even here the weave creates a smaller pattern that relates to the shirt and the sport coat.

The outfit is totally conceived, and not everyone has the talent to execute such careful coordination. That's why the ensemble is ingenious: it's individual and personal, deftly styled. Clothing: Dimitri. Model: Dan Cahill.

you do increase your chances of landing a job compatible with your nature. And that increases your chances of being content in the job, since you won't continually be forced to suppress your natural instincts. On the other hand, projecting a false identity—like claiming false credentials—can get you into ticklish situations that aren't fun or funny.

Naturally, you wear on-duty garb for more than getting a job. In many cases, if you don't continue wearing on-duty attire while conducting business, you may lose your position. Yet the principle remains the same: when you dress to highlight your abilities and your particular nature, you will be more at ease, and consequently more genuinely satisfied, than you would be while displaying a false facade.

INNER WORKINGS

The most complex on-duty style is the one called Ingenious! This complexity arises because ingeniousness is a combination of several traits in shifting, unequal proportions. Cleverness is presupposed.

So is a certain amount of unorthodoxy as well as creativity. An ingenious individual is inventive and intuitive, looks for new solutions to old problems, is resourceful and uninhibited, not bound to custom. He is not a follower, but he's not necessarily a leader. Hearing his own drummer, he moves to his own beat and refuses to alter his tempo to that of the group. He can inspire awe, respect, loyalty, envy, distrust, occasionally hostility. His self-reliance can be acclaimed as proof of his superiority or disdained as a sign of self-importance: others can think him "a whiz" or "a wise guy, too smart for his own good." But an ingenious person is rarely mistaken for a clod.

Strictly speaking, the ingenious style isn't only one way of dressing; it's an amalgam of various approaches, none of them ordinary, and responses to it are seldom indifferent. Unexpectedness is its only expectable quality. The appeal of the ingenious mode is its illusiveness and the fact that not every guy possesses the know-how to put it together.

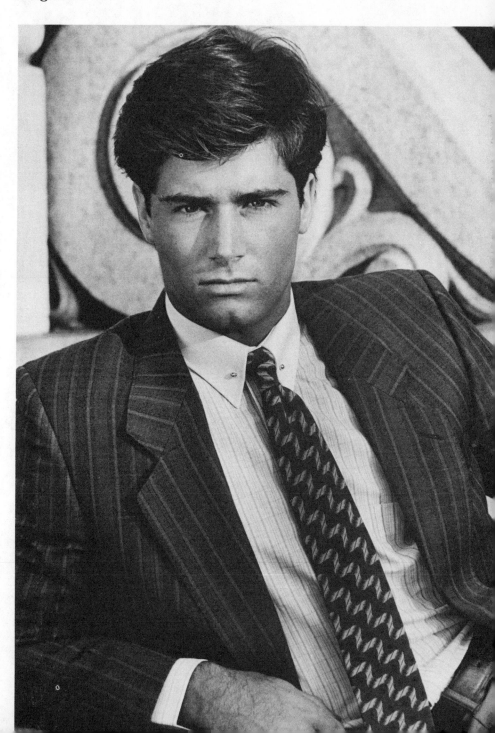

RIGHT. Aesthetics is not an exact study. What is considered visually pleasing during one period may be thought unappealing during another. This is definitely true of the aesthetics of mixing patterns in male attire. Generally, though, to achieve pleasing effects one seeks to integrate different patterns rather than tossing them in disjointedly.

These three distinctive patterns work together because, though it is not immediately apparent, they are very closely related and therefore integrate well.

While at first the sport coat appears to be vertically striped, it has enough horizontal movement in its weave to suggest a very subtle plaid.

Although the differing widths of the stripes in the coat seem almost random, the palest striped bands are placed at consistently regular intervals.

The pattern of the dress shirt, nominally a plaid, is more pronounced vertically, and the placement of the stripes echoes the feeling of the sport coat.

The undulating "stripes" of the tie pick up on the same motif.

So instead of being a motley collection of patterns, these combine for a singularity of purpose—to present an intriguing but cohesive togetherness. Jacket: Tiger of Sweden. Tie: Giorgio Armani. Shirt: Henry Grethel. Model: Lou LaRusso.

NOTS LANDING

Let's begin the explication of the ingenious style by defining what it's not. As mentioned, it's not expected, but it's not bizarre or outlandish, since no on-duty garb can ever afford to be off-the-wall. Yet it follows no rules other than those of "good taste"—a less than precise subject.

Perhaps the best way to describe the ingenious mode is to say that it always looks *new,* but not so new as to appear totally radical. Remember, we're still in the sphere of on-duty garb. The outfit must look new *and* tasteful. When you're attired in an ingenious way, you always look "well dressed." It's possible some people will accuse you of being a dandy, but you won't go unnoticed. In fact, that's the whole point of the ingenious style—to be noticed, to emerge from anonymity, to prove that you're savvy, a free spirit.

One last not: the ingenious style is not in any way pedestrian. To soar, you must test your wings.

TAKING OFF

Because ingenious clothing must look tastefully "new" in some way, to make an ingenious impression you're better off buying garments that are untraditional but not trendy. For ease of understanding, let's use an example from women's fashion to explain why.

During the 1960s, miniskirts were first trendy, later commonplace and finally unfashionable—the standard cycle for any trend that ever becomes very popular. By the middle of the 1970s, miniskirts were not the mode. When a woman wore a miniskirt then, she was thought to be wearing an outmoded style, not a new or even current one. Consequently, instead of being perceived as tastefully well dressed, she was considered poorly dressed in a style behind the times.

Let's continue with this example of the miniskirt. Let's say that at the zenith of the miniskirt craze there was a woman who bought a skirt that was very unusual for the times—one that stopped just below her knees and that was made of a handwoven tweed fabric like no other. It was a very beautiful skirt, and when she wore it, although she was not trendy, she looked "tasteful" and "new." When the miniskirt succumbed to the short-lived maxiskirt trend, whenever she wore her beautiful handwoven skirt, she looked to people who had never seen her or it before tastefully new if not trendy. Today, to strangers, she and her skirt still look both "new" and "tasteful"—in other words, ingenious.

On the other hand, if that particular skirt were to have been mass-produced and widely popular with other women at any point along the way, the scenario could not have been the same, because then the skirt would have been perceived and judged differently.

Since we never know at the outset of a trend whether it will flame or fizzle, therein lies the danger of buying trendy clothes: should they become widely popular, at some point they will lose their claim to newness. By contrast, highly unusual but nontrendy attire retains its newness as long as it is not worn by a sizable number of people.

There is a rub, of course. Unless you're a devout disciple of Fashion, you may not be able to distinguish what's truly unique from what's merely unusual. Otherwise, what looks unusual today may become trendy tomorrow, extremely popular next year and passé in another few years. More positively, however, if you catch on to an unusual look early in its evolutionary cycle, you will appear ingenious

OPPOSITE PAGE. Designers have been utilizing unusual pattern mixes more and more in recent years. When putting together their collections, they spend great amounts of time carefully coordinating fabrics to achieve total integration.

This outfit is aburst with pattern. Some will find the result exhilarating. Others will find it incomprehensible. That is always the risk of wearing highly styled ensembles.

Should you want to embark on such an adventurous route, initially you will probably find it easier to purchase an outfit already preassembled by one creator rather than attempting to collect several patterns from diverse sources.

With time and concentration, it is possible to learn the trick of pattern coordination by watching how the masters put their own looks together. Outfit: Nino Cerruti. Model: Brian Terrell.

ABOVE. Although this padded-shoulder sport coat could conceivably be mixed with other patterns, the strong and wide stripes are very distinctive in their own right, particularly so when worn with a sweater instead of the more usual dress shirt and tie, and with those unconventional pants, piped down the sides with leather.

Business associates may not approve of someone's dressing in this highly individualistic manner, but no one can say the outfit isn't ingenious. Clothing: Andrew Fezza. Model: Charlie Melite. Hairstyling: Kent Rulon.

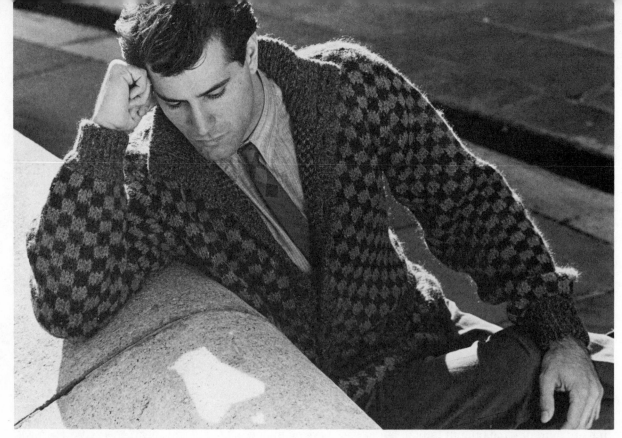

longer than someone who takes it on once it has reached a degree of popularity . . . and is losing its ingeniousness. And maybe the atypical attire will never be embraced by the multitude. Then, your ingenious impression can go on and on. The more atypical the garments you buy, the more likely they will remain atypical over the years. Of course, that also means you're potentially courting more disfavor in some people's eyes for a longer period of time. Those are the breaks. You have to weigh the risks and the rewards. In some situations, you may decide that projecting ingeniousness carries no premium. In some others, you may want to convey ingeniousness to the very limit. You're not always the master of your fate, but you can master the art of communicating purposefully and expressively in your clothing.

STOCK EXCHANGE

Failure to wear certain garments strongly identified with the conduct of business is a sure way to appear unconventional in an on-duty milieu. In many settings, neckties are noteworthy when absent. Wearing a cardigan sweater in place of a suit or sport coat is unexpected. In general, the more casual elements appear in an on-duty outfit, the more unconventional will be the impression. But ingeniousness isn't simply a matter of appearing casual. Ingeniousness is the opposite of rigid traditionalism. It can be accomplished in several ways.

SHAPE

As previously noted, if you wear unconventionally shaped attire, you will always appear to have purposefully decided to dress unusually. In the on-duty sphere, the American natural-shoulder suit is the tra-

ABOVE. When suits or sport coats aren't obligatory, but when most men appear in them, wearing a cardigan sweater and necktie will be seen as ingenious, particularly when the sweater is novel in its own right.

This one is graphically a winner and would remain so even if a traditional shirt and tie were worn with it. But to elevate the sum even higher, here you see a softly textured shirt and a fashionably thin tie with diamond shapes of the same size as the checks on the sweater.

Because the necktie is in a woven fabric and the sweater is knitted, and because different but compatible colors are employed in the tie and sweater, the result is much more stylish—and ingenious—than if the colors matched.

Coordinating colors and textures that are exactly the same from piece to piece can suggest paint-by-number simplemindedness instead of sophisticated art. Sweater: Missoni. Tie: Vicky Davis. Shirt: Giorgio Armani. Model: Michael Principe.

ditional standard for appropriate business attire. Thus, any suit *not* of this type is seen as unconventional. A wide-shouldered, narrow-waisted, hip-tight European suit coat, for instance, though hardly outrageous, will still appear quite unconventionally shaped by comparison with the natural-shoulder one. Even more unusual in the on-duty world are sport coats with very exaggerated padded shoulders and voluminous body proportions more suggestive of outerwear (according to conventional perception) than of "business clothes." Similarly, since traditional suit trousers come with straight legs, any other cut will appear to be nontraditional, and pants very roomy in the thighs and pegged to narrow cuffs will seem *very* unconventionally shaped.

Whereas a man wearing a traditional suit often looks as if he has not given careful or original thought to his clothing, making an appearance in nontraditionally shaped clothing always suggests premeditation. The more the shape of on-duty garb deviates from the conventional norm, the greater is the impression that this deviation is purposeful, far from accidental, and that a great deal of thought has gone into the decision to dress this way: a businessman wearing extremely unconventionally shaped clothing is willfully going against the traditional grain. This deliberate visual assertiveness is one way to suggest ingeniousness.

But unconventionally shaped garments seldom combine according to the rules of harmony and symmetry as outlined in the Reliable!

RIGHT. This sport coat is atypical in several ways, some more readily apparent than others. Most obvious is the kinetic pattern, creating an optical illusion of perpetual motion.

Although the eye may not consciously register the fact, the V-notch of the lapel is lower on the chest than is customary in the American natural-shoulder style (of which this is not an example), and the button closure is much closer to the waistline, creating an elongated opening above the closure between the lapels.

The shoulders have been engineered and subtly padded for more width than in traditional suits or sport coats, and the armholes are higher, the "skirt" of the jacket slightly shaped to the waist.

Even though an onlooker may not be able to articulate why, he or she will perceive these distinctions subconsciously and will pay greater attention to the sport coat than if it were styled more conventionally. This increased attention span will bring the leather pants into sharper focus.

The scooped neck of the sweater reveals the relatively small knot of the necktie—appropriate with these distinctively shaped lapels, though perhaps too small for a reliable sport coat with higher V-notches. Outfit: Giorgio Armani. Model: Eigil Dag Vesti.

chapter. An avant-garde suit coat, for example, may come with a specialized lapel treatment, perhaps suggestive of a diamond instead of the more usual V-notch; in which case you could not automatically assume that the necktie to wear should be matched in maximum width to the widest part of the diamond lapel. In all probability, such a necktie would look too wide with the suit coat because it would smother the shirt beneath it. Similarly, the reliable Reliable! rule that shirt collars should be slightly shorter than the width of the lapels wouldn't apply here either: the collar should be relatively short and the necktie relatively narrow to look their best with this avant-garde suit coat. To further complicate the matter, the shirt and the necktie shouldn't be of conventional sorts anyway, because they would look mismatched with the highly unconventional spirit of the suit coat.

Unconventionally shaped garments, while they do a very good job of imparting an ingenious aura, do pose logistical problems. Since the standard guidelines don't apply, you are forced to rely on your instincts to determine the correct proportions of the pieces. If your instincts are good, great. If they're not, the result may be not so great. But there is solace. Since conventional clothing wisdom is inapplicable here, no one can prove you're wrong whichever way you arrange the atypically shaped pieces. There are no maps when you're pioneering in untrodden territory.

And atypically cut clothing does have one singular advantage: it requires little assist to proclaim ingeniousness. Unusually shaped garments—even ones in basic colors—can be made of smooth, unpatterned fabrics and their ingeniousness won't necessarily be diminished. If garments are cut traditionally, however, either their textures, their colors or their patterns must be unusually untraditional when you're set on an ingenious impression.

TEXTURE

The role texture plays in imparting ingeniousness changes according to the character of the garments assembled. When traditionally shaped garments are colored or patterned in very innovative ways, they project some degree of ingeniousness even if their textures are standard smooth ones. However, if traditionally shaped garments are also colored or patterned traditionally, texture remains the sole means to inject ingeniousness. In this case, at least one atypical texture is called for. Generally, an outfit that combines several tactile textures is more ingenious than one combining several smooth ones *if* the shapes and colors or patterns of the garments are the same. But untraditionally cut and colored garments in smooth textures will look more ingenious than traditionally cut and colored garments in tactile textures. In other words, no one type of texture is automatically more or less ingenious than any other. But when all is said and done, although strong textures are not imperative in this mode, they tend to afford you a head start in projecting ingeniousness.

COLOR

You may have realized by now that the ingenious on-duty style bears some similarities to the off-duty styles called Earthy! and Smart! They too are highly individualistic, and both often utilize color in adventurous ways. Review the color principles in those chapters to apply them to ingenious on-duty garb. However, since we're now discussing on-duty garb, remember that greater innovation in color is allowable in the off-duty realm. Extremely emotional hues are mostly incompati-

RIGHT. To many, this outfit will appear avant-garde, even though it was designed several years ago—proof that purchasing highly original clothing that is outside the mainstream increases the possibility of appearing original for a long period of time: onlookers uninvolved with the fashion industry seldom are aware of seasonal changes in "forward fashion" and, being unable to pinpoint when an innovation occurs, tend to consider all unconventional but aesthetically pleasing outfits ingeniously "new."

Notice the unusual lapels here. Because they come to a point without any notched opening, they are called "diamond" lapels. (Imagine the lapels joined side by side; they would then form a diamond shape.) Only a small percentage of suits with diamond lapels are made each year. Many stores never offer any, so few people are familiar with them.

A man who wears a diamond-lapel suit will invariably be singled out for attention, will be looked over, never overlooked.

But some men, lacking familiarity with the style, might accessorize the suit conventionally, and that would detract from its aesthetics. The "right" shirt and tie—"right" because that's the way the designer conceived the total look—have trimmer dimensions than conventional dress shirts and ties. The collar, for instance, has fairly short points, and the knitted tie is narrowish.

While the diamond lapels are very innovative, innovation is also present in the shaped-to-the-body, relatively short jacket with widened shoulders.

The texture is also untraditional—an extremely tactile chenille.

And the color, mixed from several yarns, is an offbeat shade between teal blue and teal green.

With innovation so marked, this outfit is ingenious indeed. Outfit: Jhane Barnes. Model: Stuart Carberry.

ble with suits, so when they're employed (if at all), it's best to confine them to other items, such as neckties, pocket squares or sweater vests.

Although unusually shaped clothing needs no bolstering from offbeat color to maintain its ingenious quality, offbeat colors in combination with unusual shapes and textures compound ingeniousness.

PATTERN

Since the ingenious mode embraces a number of unpredictable looks, pattern can be used in a variety of ways . . . or may not be employed at all. A solid teal blue sport coat, steel gray trousers, a lavender dress shirt and a solid indigo necktie make up an ingenious outfit without a pattern in sight. Exchange the sport coat for one striped in teal blue, pewter gray and mauve without replacing any of the other pieces and the outfit is still ingenious, *not* because of the striping but because of the colorful interplay between all the garments. Patterns can help inject ingeniousness, but they're not mandatory *unless* the pieces are all conventional in shape, color and texture, in which case only an infusion of pattern can supply touches of ingeniousness.

Although patterns aren't requisite to the ingenious style, and while ingeniousness can be attained without a resort to patterns, mixing patterned components is one definite way to impart ingeniousness. Thus, patterns in concert with other patterns appear more regularly in the ingenious style than in the other on-duty modes. To keep the patterns from fighting each other, careful attention must be given to coordinating their scales and their colors. It is virtually impossible to mix three or more large-scaled, vividly colored patterns. Smaller-scaled patterns in vivid hues are more manageable, particularly if buffered with less intense or neutral shades. A knit garment, such as a sweater vest, helps subdue the combativeness that can rear up among several patterned woven fabrics.

PARALLEL LINES

Since ingeniousness can be achieved in divergent ways, it's impossible to single out individual garments representative of the style. A suit that by itself might be considered the height of reliability, for instance, can be paired with other articles in ways that will make the

BOTH LEFT. Although individual garments may not be especially innovative, sometimes the mixture of such items can be atypical and will therefore suggest ingeniousness.

This sport coat is more conventional than the one with diamond lapels shown on the preceding page. Here you see the more standard V-notch lapels.

The shoulders are slightly built up in the European manner, but not exaggeratedly so.

Plaid patterns are not unfamiliar in on-duty attire, although this one contains rich blue-purple and rose.

Most distinguishing in the sport coat is the luster of the iridescent fabric.

The shirt, the necktie and the pants aren't fundamentally innovative either. Although its scale is on the large side, the shirt pattern is a classic tattersall, with a pastel pink ground. The tie has a dusty lavender background but otherwise isn't truly noteworthy. And the gray-blue pants, although pleated stylishly, aren't detailed in any way to cause heads to turn.

The outfit's ingeniousness arises from the atypical interplay of the less-than-ingenious individual parts. Thus, although the impression conveyed is definitely ingenious, it is more understated than if each garment had been extraordinary in its own right.

As presented, the pattern mix is most responsible for conveying ingeniousness, with assistance also coming from the somewhat offbeat colors. Sport coat & pants: Ermenegildo Zegna. Shirt: Lee Wright. Model: Tom Tripodi. Hairstyling: Kent Rulon.

overall impression ingenious. Unfortunately, a suit that by itself might be considered extremely ingenious can also be paired with other articles in ways that will render the overall impression tasteless. So, recognizing this, let's try to compile a few guidelines for building an ingenious wardrobe.

SUITS

Since traditionally shaped natural-shoulder suits are strongly identified with both the Reliable! and the Sincere! modes, they lack inherent ingeniousness and will always appear less ingenious than a suit with an unorthodox shape. However, a traditionally shaped suit can still project an ingenious look. If you want to appear only somewhat ingenious, veer toward a conventional suit in a fairly traditional fabric in a slightly unusual color—say, a heathered flannel or an unemphatic tweed suit in a taupe tone—so that it can be combined with conventional ingredients (a white shirt and a narrowly striped silk tie, for example) when a conservative impression is desired or with unconventional ingredients (for instance, a pale green-and-pink plaid shirt, a forest green bow tie and a claret sweater vest) when you want to convey more ingeniousness.

Of course, middle ground does exist between suits that are strongly traditional and those that are avant-garde. Take the matter of lapels. The V-notch lapel is the most customary in men's suits. Peaked lapels—lapels with an upward slant, coming to a point (peak) with the collar; only a narrow, slanted space is left between the collar and the lapels—are a staple lapel style, particularly in double-breasted suits. Peaked lapels are not so uncustomary as to appear strange, but are not seen regularly enough to seem commonplace. Thus, most suits with peaked lapels begin with a touch of ingeniousness. When they're colored or textured unusually, they proclaim more of the trait.

In a more avant-garde vein are suits that simply don't look the way most suits do. Some of these have coats that are hybrids between suit coats and outerwear. They are still "suits" because the same fabric is used for both the coat and the trousers. Such "suits," because of their unorthodox shapes, are attention-grabbing and therefore ingenious, but they may be frowned upon in conservative professional situations. When such avant-garde concoctions are to be worn in place of standard business attire, it is wiser to select them in neutral or traditionally masculine colors. In milieus more liberal and creative, all barriers drop.

SPORT COATS

As with suits, conventional sport coats can't initiate an ingenious impression, but when the other components are selected with ingeniousness in mind, they can be part of a team effort to convey the characteristic.

Take a classic blue blazer. If it is worn with full-cut, highly tactile tweed pants, a multicolored striped shirt with a pale pastel rounded collar and an offbeat foulard necktie, plus bright suspenders and two-tone canvas shoes without socks—that's ingenious. Yet the classic blue blazer is still intrinsically traditional; it has assumed an aura of ingeniousness as if by osmosis, by drawing the trait from the surrounding articles. Thus, greater pressure is placed on the supporting garments to be very ingenious in order for the blazer to "absorb" their ingeniousness. If an ingenious sport coat had been selected in the first place, it would not have been as incumbent on all the other pieces of the outfit to rank high in ingeniousness.

While a classic blue blazer isn't inherently ingenious, a blazer striped in bands of rust, brown and camel is automatically the more ingenious of the two. Similarly, most large-scaled patterns are more ingenious than moderately scaled ones on sport coats of the same basic shape.

In some instances, so-called "shirt jackets" are worn in place of more authentic sport coats. This substitution is a more innovative sign of ingeniousness. When the shirt jacket is also innovatively colored or patterned or textured—or all three—gradations of ingeniousness are increased.

As a general rule, substitution of a less likely, entirely different garment (say, a satin baseball jacket) for a more customary one (such as a traditional blue blazer) is the most pronounced way to assert ingeniousness. And not everyone will approve of the substitution. Beware juxtapositions that can appear incongruous.

DRESS PANTS

The story with dress pants is similar to the tale of sport coats: conventional dress pants won't stop you from making an ingenious impression, but unconventional trousers start you out more surely. Naturally, unconventionality has many expressions.

Brightly colored or largely patterned pants—ones you might think of as being ingenious—are so strongly associated with off-duty garb that most critics stubbornly rebel against accepting them in an on-duty context. Atypically shaped but moderately colored or patterned

trousers are generally the more acceptable alternative for projecting ingeniousness. Strong textures are likewise preferable to overly strong colors, particularly the emotional hues.

The reason onlookers are more finicky about pants than about other garment classifications is that trousers represent sexual territory: men must wear *the* pants; and if they're not the right pants, a man is not thought to be a rightful male, particularly in the on-duty world. For this reason, shorts are verboten in on-duty transactions . . . unless you're a mailman or someone employed in menial labor. Or unless you're a true-blue iconoclast. Even lore-laden leather pants are favored above Bermuda shorts in the workaday setting where it's more permissible to wear sexually tinged skin substitutes than to expose the real thing. In the on-duty scheme of things, the less human flesh exposed the better.

DRESS SHIRTS

Because the sight of human flesh is nearly anathema on on-duty turf, short-sleeved shirts are off limits. Otherwise, the more you deviate from conventional dress shirts, the more ingenious will be your impression, provided you don't overstep into fabrics relegated only for female consumption; a lace shirt is a no-no.

Depending upon your chosen route to project ingeniousness, you can avoid the guise of the conventional dress shirt in different ways. One method is simply to opt for highly unconventional colors. Since white and pale pastels are the hues most visible in conventional dress shirts, mid-toned and dark shades in standard shapes and textures transmit ingeniousness. The more unstandard the shape and texture of the shirt, the greater the degree of ingeniousness conveyed by a mid-toned or dark-colored shirt. High dramatic content is one sure signal of ingeniousness.

Distinctive patterning is another way of transforming the conventional dress shirt into an unconventional one. As already noted, mixing patterns with other patterns is always perceived as a sign of ingeniousness . . . as long as the patterns work in concert.

Collar treatments can also contribute to ingeniousness. Spread

BELOW. There's no way this outfit could be considered an on-duty ensemble; shorts—even a conservative pair like these—just don't make the grade in professional circles.

The outfit does prove, however, that clothing from one realm can be reassembled with articles from another to express a new perspective.

As shown with the shorts, the ensemble is designed to poke fun at very serious dress by parodying it.

Now imagine a pair of chino slacks instead of the shorts. Then the outfit would be lightheartedly ingenious because of the pattern mix and the bow tie.

But if the shorts were exchanged for a pair of dark gabardine slacks, the effect would be more serious, but still not completely so: bow ties, particularly those in pale hues, are low in formality (except when worn at formal events with formal gear), so they always reduce an outfit's authority. Outfit (excepting tie): Sahara Club. Tie: Vicky Davis. Model: Bill Sullivan.

If shorts were worn here and not the flannel pants, the outfit would be in the same league as the one on the opposite page. Given the flannel dress pants, however, the effect is more sophisticatedly ingenious than that opposite outfit would be with long pants.

Why? The vest, of course, patterned with fishing-tackle flies.

When fabric vests match a suit (or sport coat), they usually increase authority. When nonmatching, they assume greater decorative importance.

The more decorative nonmatching vests become, the more ingenious they appear. This one has a deep red background for extra visibility and panache.

Notice the way a fractional glimpse of the shirt cuff is visible below the cuff of the sport coat. Although this is not necessarily the case, more shirt cuff may be exposed when outfits are on the dressy side than with less dressy attire. Under no circumstances, however, should much more than half an inch be seen. Outfit: Alan Flusser. Model: John Sommi. Hairstyling: Kent Rulon. Background fabric: Lee-Joffa.

collars—those which are shortish in length and wider between their points than usual—are generally considered more elegant than button-down or conventional pointed collars. This reputed elegance is why they are considered ingenious. Rounded collars are given similar accord. Ditto for contrasting collars, colored differently from the body of the shirt. All three of these collar styles are usually worn with neckties and may look odd without them.

Sportier shirts can also look ingenious, but not if the other components are highly dressy, since then juxtaposition gives way to incongruity. A plaid flannel sport shirt worn with roomily proportioned wide-waled corduroy pants, a bulky cardigan sweater and a slender leather tie represents an ingenious outfit, but the same shirt worn with a pin-striped suit doesn't because of the incongruity, with or without the leather or any other necktie.

SWEATERS

Although sweaters are normally thought of as casual attire, their use as on-duty garb can be seen as an ingenious step. Consider what happens when a conventional business look composed of a blue blazer, white shirt, striped tie and gray flannel pants is altered by the addition of any sweater, be it a V-neck, a crew-neck or one styled with a distinctive collar to expose some of the shirt collar and the knot of the necktie. Naturally, the more ingenious the sweater in shape, color, pattern or texture, the more ingenious will be the impression; but simply adding a sweater is an advance toward ingeniousness. Additional touches can accelerate the sense of ingeniousness—adding a colorful belt, inserting a patterned square into the breast pocket of the blazer, topping it all off with a jaunty straw hat with a decorative hatband—to such a degree that the sweater can even be removed without diminishing the newfound ingeniousness achieved from the new innovative pieces. Still, while sweaters are not obliga-

tory in making an ingenious impression, they are helpful when you're faced with limited choices among other components.

NECKTIES

Bow ties are not widely worn and therefore draw attention to themselves, thereby suggesting ingeniousness when the rest of the outfit has only limited innovation. Per usual, the more unconventional other garments in an outfit are, the more ingenious will be the impression abetted by the bow tie. But bow ties aren't the only ingenious neckwear. Offbeat color, texture and pattern can be found in conventional neckties too. And don't forget about shape (in the case of neckties other than bow ties, meaning width).

Traditional neckwear differs from today's "fashion" neckties in that the latter are often narrower, from slightly to a lot. Since fashionability may be considered by many to be interchangeable with ingeniousness, a narrow "fashion" necktie need not conform to conventional rules to look "right." Thus, in highly styled ingenious outfits, neckties may often be narrower than customary. This is not absolutely mandatory but is a sometime fact. Similarly, neckties worn with the elegant collar treatments—the spread, rounded and contrast collars—also tend to be slightly—or greatly, depending upon one's taste—narrower than those seen in the Reliable! or even the Sincere! styles.

Jewelry associated with neckwear is another sign of ingeniousness. Metal collar pins that attach to the shirt collar to hold it in place—or simply to be there for show—are a case in point. Tie clasps and tacks are also worn more for ingeniousness than for reliability or sincerity.

FOOTWEAR

Decorative shoe styles are more ingenious than "sensible" ones. Thick soles are too high on practicality to be ingenious. Ingenious shoes are often sleekly dressy, although in more casual ingenious outfits, decidedly casual styling is acceptable—but *not* jogging shoes.

OUTERWEAR

As with footwear, practicality and ingeniousness are at odds with each other. This does not mean that warmth is not a consideration; it's just not the first consideration—style is. Therefore, a conventional trench coat is not in the ingenious mode. But a voluminous trench coat in an atypical color—say, an olive drab hue; lined in another color—perhaps black or midnight brown—is. Or imagine an overcoat architectural in its simplicity but made up in an intricately woven tweed. It too is ingenious because *style,* not creature comfort, is the overriding factor.

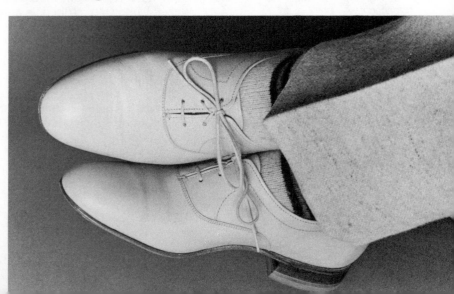

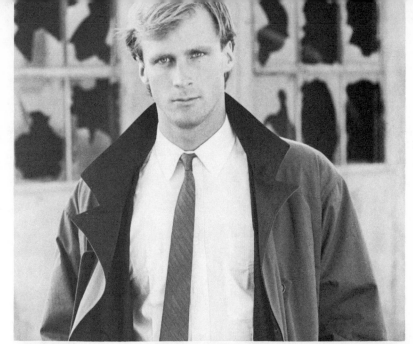

UPPER LEFT. *In some settings, the lack of a necktie might disqualify this outfit from being considered on-duty apparel. But if the ensemble were worn by a real estate agent showing a condominium, you couldn't say these are play togs. In fact, the outfit is more upscale than the clothing worn by many professional men who aren't obliged to wear suits and ties.*

If the sweater were removed and a conventional dress shirt added without a tie, the result would be unstylishly commonplace. The sweater helps the outfit ascend to new heights of ingeniousness. Clothing: Ferragamo. Model (below as well): Timothy Doshier.

MIDDLE LEFT. *The sport coat is handsome but not charged with innovative energy. Ditto for the pants.*

But both the shirt and tie are innovative—the shirt because it has a small "fashion" collar and the tie because it is narrow and therefore a "fashion" sort. Outfit: Ermenegildo Zegna. Tie: Rooster.

LOWER LEFT. *These are called "jazz" shoes, and that name tells you they are not standard for business, which is why they are ingenious when selected for on-duty purposes.*

The bone color goes well with the "winter white" trousers.

In keeping with these tones, the socks are mostly pale with unusual horizontal stripes.

Dark shoes would be jarring to the eye and unnecessarily heavy.

UPPER RIGHT. *This raincoat is gracefully proportioned, but that doesn't earn its ingenious reputation. The "fashion" collar does, and the fact that the coat is olive green lined in midnight brown. Coat: Hugo Boss. Necktie: Punch. Model: David Hopkins.*

LOWER RIGHT. *By contrast to the one above, this quilted raincoat doesn't "drape" on the body. Its dramatic proportions explain its ingeniousness. Coat: Charivari Men. Model: Brian Terrell.*

ACCESSORIES

Since ingeniousness culls diverse recourses, accessories play a big part in putting together an ingenious look, especially when the accessories contain an element of surprise. Suspenders can be a bracing addition. Inserting an antique cuff link into the buttonhole of a suit coat's lapel is an unpredictable—and ingenious—touch. So is puffing two solid-colored squares into the suit coat's breast pocket so that onlookers see two color charges instead of one. Since unpredictability is the only predictable factor in the ingenious style, minor touches add up to major importance.

ROLE CALL

Since there are many ways to impart ingeniousness, the mode can be modified in many ways. In mainly conservative professional fields, an ingenious look, as we've seen, can even revolve around a traditionally shaped natural-shoulder business suit. But the most ingeniously put-together outfit for the sphere of high finance, based on a conventional suit, will appear less ingenious than one based on an avant-garde suit assembled for the milieu of the rock-music industry, where extreme innovation is expected. But whatever the setting, the

LEFT. This striated striped suit comes in subtle iridescent colors. The shirt has a white spread collar—tastefully held in place by a gold collar bar—and a very pale yellow body. The paisley-patterned silk tie is multicolored in pastels.

Already ingenious, the outfit becomes more so with one final touch: placing a sprig of dried statice in the buttonhole of the lapel. Suit: Ermenegildo Zegna. Shirt: Ron Chereskin. Model: John Sommi. Hairstyling: Kent Rulon.

RIGHT. Spread-collar shirts have gained popularity with menswear designers in recent years because their elegant proportions help "dress up" outfits and allow greater color expression in the shirting fabrics without sacrificing "class."

This spread-collar shirt contains more colorful stripes than those customary in dress shirts, and the stripes are unusual in another way too: they are not symmetrical from the left side of the chest to the right. In fact, the color placement in the shirt, like that of the necktie, doesn't repeat itself regularly and is therefore unpredictable. This unpredictability indicates ingeniousness.

So does the way the pocket square picks up the purple and red shades found in the shirt, tie and sport coat. Since pocket squares are not handkerchiefs but nonfunctional pieces of decoration, they are not removed in public. For this reason, if they are "puffed" into the pocket like this, with no edges showing, you can save money by purchasing snippets of fabric and using them as pocket squares instead of shelling out more dough for authentic ones with finished edges. Outfit: Alexander Julian. Model: Henry Mellen.

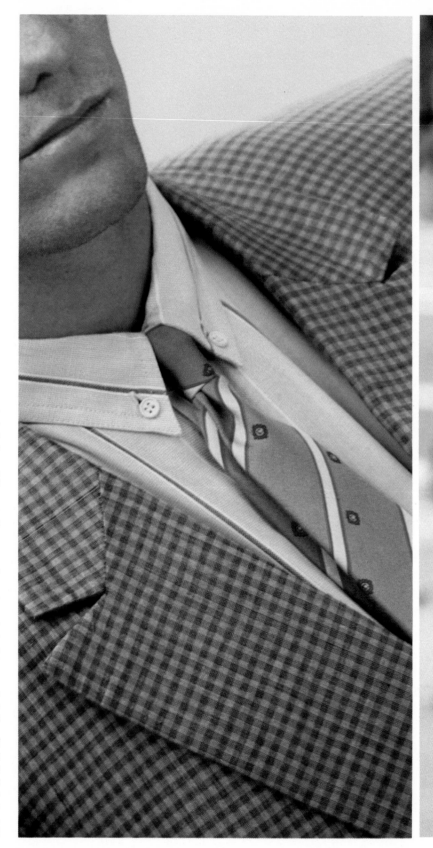

NEAR & MIDDLE RIGHT. The lapels of this sport coat are an unusual cross between peaked and V-notched lapels, so their shape alone conveys ingeniousness. But the colors and the mixture of patterns are also atypical in on-duty apparel, compounding the sense of ingeniousness.

Notice how the sport coat, dress shirt and necktie all contain gray and pink in only slightly different shades. Using compatible colors from garment to garment is one sure way to coordinate patterns well.

Although these pieces look ingenious together, their scales are arranged according to the traditional rule: when three patterns are mixed, three different scales are generally preferred.

In this case, the check of the coat is the small-scaled one, the shirt is striped in a medium scale and the tie is the large-scaled pattern. Model: Jim Foulk.

FAR RIGHT. Very tactile fabrics in interesting weaves express ingeniousness, and that's why this outfit looks as ingenious as it does.

With numerous yarns of assorted but closely related hues appearing in both the jacket and tie, the presence of a fairly conventional—albeit pink—dress shirt dispels none of the ingenious appeal while rooting the ensemble firmly in on-duty ground. Clothing: Jhane Barnes. Model: Quentin Hunt.

LEFT. A spritely tie can take center stage. When it does, but if the other elements in an outfit are bland, the tie can be accused of overacting.

When the other pieces provide interesting but secondary support, however, the tie receives greater critical acclaim because it becomes an integral, if stellar, part of the whole. Such is the case here.

Although the necktie boldly advances, the nubby checked suit coat and the plaid dress shirt hold their own and don't disappear from view. The man doesn't come across as a "walking necktie," but as a natty individual who pays attention to all details, including the square in the breast pocket. Clothing: Alexander Julian. Model: Jim Catch.

RIGHT. Here is another totally conceived outfit, even though one garment—this time the sweater vest, with an ingenious dark-colored dress shirt beneath it—has the upper hand.

All else being equal, the garment with the most pronounced pattern commands more attention than those patterned on a smaller scale.

But all else is seldom equal.

Sport coats are bigger in volume than sweater vests, and they cut down on the latter's visibility and impact.

If the patterns were reversed here —if the sport coat were made in a contrasting geometric pattern and the sweater vest were of a tactile but essentially solid material—then the sport coat would command so much attention as to become overpowering.

Since emphatic patterns, like emphatic colors, become more and more emphatic as the volume of the garments they're found on increases, it is often a tasteful decision to confine their appearance to relatively small garments.

Mid-toned or darkly colored garments also help to tame the effect of very pronounced patterns. If these pants were white, for example, the outfit would jump forward more than it does. Hyperactivity is seldom desirable in on-duty apparel.

As an aside, if you ever try the ingenious ploy of wearing a belt on a pair of pants that fails to supply loops, try to make certain the belt remains on the waistband and doesn't slip above it. This is not an easy thing to do. Clothing: Cesarani. Model: Neil Kramer.

principles of dressing ingeniously hold true: the outfit must look *new* and *tasteful,* according to the standards of the crowd.

When you walk into a men's-clothing store to buy something very special, do you approach a salesperson who is clothed in a humdrum manner or one who emanates a deft sense of style? The latter, of course, because that deftness of style convinces you the advice you'll receive is worth listening to—at least on subjects of "taste," though maybe not in the area of stocks and bonds.

The analogy to a salesperson in a men's store is purposeful, because there knowledge based on "taste" is high on the priority list. The ingenious style "sells" its wearer by subliminally telling viewers that the man has creative insights and a finely tuned sensibility, a sophisticated outlook. When such qualities are greatly prized, dressing ingeniously is an asset. When people are seeking assistance on purely practical matters, dressing ingeniously can be a detriment. That's why ingeniousness must always be tempered to the situation.

Because the ingenious style relies upon strong visual stimuli, it is not restful to the eye. Charged with energy, the mode is dynamic, never static. It is busy with small touches and extra little details. Its vitality, if it's poorly executed, can be mistaken for disorganized disarray. Even when the style is properly executed, some may still think it overworked and overly self-conscious. You must have the courage of your convictions to carry off the ingenious mode. On the other hand, when you dress and act with conviction, the courageous style can help you make many conquests, professional and otherwise.

CHAPTER 11
POWERFUL!

TOUGH STRATEGY

Power misused is power abused. In a utopian world, power is exercised only for the right, and might never *makes* right.

Now let's descend to the real world. Often those who are believed to possess power hold powerful sway. Many follow the powerful unquestioningly. The semblance of power can actually imbue an individual with power, and the semblance of a truth becomes the truth.

Repeatedly you've been advised never to enlist clothing to deceive, never to ask that your garb make false claims, but to present yourself truthfully in the way you dress. While that admonition remains, it's time for a slight reassessment.

Theoretically, there is no justification for the style called Powerful! Idealistically, why would you ever choose to parade superior might before the less mighty? Is it not better to *be* powerful, modestly so, than to flaunt the trappings of power? Of course. In Utopia.

A harsh truth of the on-duty world is that, in certain circumstances at least, the failure to project a powerful impression will reduce your ability to control the situation. A brilliant general, for instance, becomes virtually powerless when he cannot command his troops because he is out of uniform. And this analogy holds true in the minefields of business: on occasion, some individuals will refuse to believe that someone possesses power, even power justly come by, and will refuse to follow the lead of the person with superior qualities and qualifications unless that someone exhibits the *appearance* of power. Thus, for purely pragmatic reasons—to get the job done—there are occasions when conveying a powerful image is desirable in the on-duty milieu.

Is it ever justifiable to *appear* powerful when one simply wants to command the same courtesy that the powerful often receive, such as winning the deferential nod from a haughty maître d' and being seated at the right spot in a restaurant? Not an easy question to

LEFT. Although the conduct of business should never descend to fisticuffs, mental and emotional sparring is inevitable. The powerful mode recognizes that all may not be peaceful in the corporate hierarchy, where dress is often used, justly or not, to intimidate. The purposeful intention of powerful attire is to suggest that a man wearing it has made his mark and is a formidable opponent. Model: Hans Lundgren.

answer. In a utopian world, favoritism would not be accorded indiscriminately to those who have a powerful air. But we already know we don't inhabit Utopia. The semblance of power can be a powerful thing.

TREASURE CHEST

Language can give clues to hidden meanings. When someone is referred to as a "man of stature," clearly he is a person of special rank and privy to power. Not so evidently, the use of the word "stature"—which also refers to the height of a person standing upright—suggests that those possessing superior physical presence also tend to possess superior power. Thus, "a man of standing" is likewise a man of special rank because of his *upright*—that is, morally and physically superior—stance. Subliminally, power is associated with the physical. Small men, whose physiques appear more powerlessly childlike than powerfully manly, have more difficulty projecting an aura of power than men of naturally greater physical "stature" and "standing."

In the animal realm, the humanlike ape asserts dominance by puffing out his chest. In the human world, man does the same, although often only symbolically. The double-breasted suit has become a potent icon of business rank because it defends the manly chest from attack by inserting an extra protective layer—an inanimate bodyguard, and only the powerful require such measures—while it also visually expands the chest so that it appears more dominant. When the double-breasted suit is darkly colored, it connotes even greater power, because dark colors have greater "weight" (that is, stature) than pale ones. Smooth textures appear more durable, hence less likely to yield, than tactile ones. Consequently, a dark-colored, smooth-surfaced double-breasted suit epitomizes power because of its formidable character. It is high on authority, low on sentiment; it exemplifies solid substance, the triumph of the physical over the emotional.

Since the possession of power also includes the ability to subjugate, it's imperative that the powerful not fall prey to emotionalism, because power can then degenerate into tyranny—power out of control. For this reason, power in the on-duty world is restricted in its imagery solely to the "objective" characteristics of manliness. Unorthodox shapes are not allowable because they are too suggestive of creativity, which is often perceived in terms of instability: the powerful must always be stable. Warm, advancing colors are impermissible, because they too are indicative of volatile sentiment: the powerful must always be cool in judgment. Tactile fabrics are inadmissible because they are woven openly and are too accessible: the powerful must always be impenetrable. In essence, powerful clothing separates the wearer from common humanity and promotes him to the superhuman. The powerful mode doesn't elicit affection; it can engender awe . . . or resentment which can lead to insubordination: the powerful must always exercise a firm hand.

PROPRIETARY INTEREST

The powerful could be a sad lot if power hadn't its rewards—often financial rewards. Money may not buy happiness, but it sure beats insolvency. The powerful are often wealthy, since wealth is also

LEFT. Power imagery is always concerned with "stature"—presenting an imposing facade. Clothing with "substance" heads the list of powerful garments, and this outfit is substantial enough for a head of state because of the relationship of all the pieces.

In shape, this suit doesn't differ from the conventional cut of reliable and sincere suits. However, its densely dark color conveys "weight." That the suit is vested also gives it a powerful boost, since extra weightiness is given to the chest.

Although the pure white shirt is often associated with reliability (which is not as potent a trait as powerfulness), here the collar is slightly spread—more elegant than a more commonplace button-down version —to suggest a man of "means."

The lustrous silk of both the tie and pocket square further indicate fineness of "taste."

The power of the outfit, then, stems from the confident, assertive mix of these various elements.

Simply exchanging the silk tie for a knitted one would disrupt the powerful concoction. Suit: Cricketeer. Shirt: Henry Grethel. Tie: Cacharel. Model: David Spiewak.

power, so the restrictions of the powerful mode do not extend to a prohibition against a show of opulence. The finesse of tailoring and fit attainable only through custom-made clothes is befitting to the style. Quality is another hallmark. For men with limited funds, the look of power is hard to achieve. It is better to purchase only a few but first-rate garments than to look like a parvenu in inferior goods. If custom-made items are unaffordable, take extra pains to find a gifted tailor to make the necessary alterations so that your clothing looks as close to custom-tailored as possible.

What are the specific garments that contribute to the power look? Depending upon how resonantly you want to declaim power, you have a choice of several expressions.

SUITS

As noted, the most powerful suit is a double-breasted one in a dark color with a smooth texture. Peaked lapels are more distinguished than those with a V-notch, so they are preferred. Black is a very heavy color, almost relentlessly so; the rich reserve of a deep navy blue carries almost as much authority as black and is not quite as forbidding. The austere gravity of very dark gray also projects power well.

As long as the shape is not avant-garde, it matters little how the suit is cut from among the various traditional styles. The body shaping associated with the British style does make the chest more emphatic, but not so greatly that the more shapeless natural-shoulder styling suffers markedly by comparison. Likewise, padded shoulders do suggest shoulders squared off for action, but this is not a major addition either.

While hard, smooth gabardine epitomizes a powerful fabric, fine flannels without an overly napped surface can also be viewed as powerful in deep colorations. Tweeds, however, almost always have too much tactility to appear powerful.

Solid fabrics are generally more powerful than patterned ones. Plaids almost never convey power unless they are very traditional, such as mini glen plaids with little color contrast. If such a plaid suit is called upon to project power, the supporting garments must be especially imbued with powerful imagery. Stripes can transmit power more directly than plaids. Pin stripes, highly identified with the Reliable! mode, can indicate a modicum of power, but chalk stripes— similar to pin stripes but thicker and more widely spaced—are more definite in their personality, thus seemingly more powerful. With their stronger presence, chalk stripes can be utilized on grounds colored paler than usual in the powerful mode without too great a diminution of power. In fact, to reduce apparent power without sacrificing the trait altogether, relatively pale chalk-striped suits are particularly helpful.

Single-breasted suits should be selected according to the same

principles as double-breasted ones, except that in most instances they should have matching vests. (Double-breasted suits are seldom vested.) Vests with lapels—yes, there are such things—should be avoided, because they smack too much of dandyism. Opulence is allowable in the powerful mode, but of the understated variety. Strong innovation is considered brash, not refined enough for the purists. Although difficult to locate, single-breasted suits with peaked lapels are a mark of distinction, not brashness, and therefore are welcome.

SPORT COATS

Sport coats are seldom worn in an on-duty setting to convey power because of their informality. Six-button, double-breasted blue blazers, however, project sizable authority and can be substituted for a suit if not on a daily basis. Similarly, tartan sport coats, though more familiar among the powerful in off-duty settings, are suffused with enough tradition to make the powerful grade . . . barely.

DRESS PANTS

Since sport coats seldom inhabit the powerful on-duty realm, there is little room for dress slacks. Only traditionally styled ones in dark or fairly dark colors can cross this border. Little texture is admissible.

DRESS SHIRTS

Casual styling is incompatible with the powerful mode, so only solid-colored or striped dress shirts in white or pale masculine hues are pure enough to portray power. Bright or dark colors are absolutely off limits. Two of the elegant shirt collars—spread and contrast—are distinguished enough to make an entry here, but the rounded collar, because roundness and womanliness are strongly linked, is barred. Button-down and standard pointed collars are too commonplace to connote power, but they are permissible when the remaining components are securely powerful.

Monograms are a sign of power and an embroidered reminder that no one should dare try to abscond with the personal garb of those in power.

NECKTIES

Youth is thought to be frivolous. A young man must be more stringent in his clothing choices to project power than a man made wise and earnest by time. An elderly man, therefore, can wear a discreet silk bow tie and be viewed as powerful, while a young man can't: on youth, the bow tie is frivolous . . . or perhaps a relic from prep-school days, proving immaturity and lack of weathered sagacity.

Since displaying one's rank—and, by extension, affluence—is integral to projecting power, richly patterned silk ties are a powerful touch, provided the patterns are not largely scaled, because they will then seem brash—a style affected by the *nouveaux riches*, not by the top-drawer powerful. Thus, small or moderate-scaled geometric, foulard and paisley prints are foremost. Stripes and solids will do in a pinch, but not knits or textural ties.

SWEATERS

Sweaters have no role in projecting power; they're too soft.

RIGHT. Power imagery includes more signs of affluence than the other on-duty modes.

Notice the show of wealth here, in the gold collar pin, the gold cuff links, the gold watch, the gold belt buckle, even to the discreet monogram on the shirt's breast pocket.

Also note that there is no flashy pinky ring with a chunky gem, which would be a sign of indiscretion.

Now look more closely at the shirt. It is finely striped with little contrast between the stripes, but the collar is white and starched. There is also a button on the shirt sleeve that is usually absent on less expensive shirts.

This button reputedly makes it easier to slip an arm through the sleeve and out the cuff without a struggle, although the truth of the matter is that afterward there's a struggle to button that button.

No matter. The powerful realm is often a precarious place. That's why the powerful exhibit the fruits of their labor by wearing opulent ties and other symbols of their exalted position as visible reminders to subordinates that they deserve respect. Model: Pat Hardie.

FAR RIGHT. Great precision is required to make "seamless" shoes, where the only visible seam is up the back of the shoe, and the extra effort shoemakers must expend makes such shoes a reward of the powerful.

Black conveys great authority, but cordovan leather seamless-toe shoes pass the powerful grade. Here the hosiery is silk—another touch of luxury that the powerful can afford.

224

FOOTWEAR

Wing-tip and cap-toe shoes have sufficient classic appeal to work in the powerful mode, but they are both brogues, fundamentally very sturdy shoes. When one occupies a position of power, subordinates do the legwork; less hardy shoes are needed. Indeed, shoes that are easily scuffed but instead are highly polished and buffed let the world know who possesses the power to wear the impractical. Seamless-toe shoes are shoes for the truly powerful. As the name indicates, these have no seams on the toe area; in fact, the entire upper (non-sole) portion of the shoe is of one piece, stitched only in the back.

But the truly powerful aren't frivolous. Their hosiery is conservatively dark and of an executive length, extending over the calf to just below the knee, so they will never commit the gaucherie of exposing their shins when crossing their legs.

OUTERWEAR

Though not frivolous or gauche, the powerful don't shy away from conspicuous consumption when what's conspicuous is considered classically tasteful. Although velvet is a soft fabric, it's also a regal one; a smidgen of velvet on an overcoat can't hurt. And that's all the velvet the Chesterfield overcoat has—a smidgen at the collar. Often with peaked lapels, it's a dressy, almost formal, topcoat. In navy blue cashmere, with black velvet for the collar but with the lapels matching the cashmere of the body, it's very, very richly powerful.

ACCESSORIES

The powerful look as if they could afford the best even when they can't. When they can't afford it, they don't purchase an inferior substitute; they go without. Tasteful solid-gold cuff links that are styled to look like buttons imply that their powerful owner has the Midas touch. He doesn't? He wears button-cuffed shirts with plastic buttons instead of French cuffs.

Even the powerful occasionally have to transport work from the office. They carry it in a fine leather attaché case that the more lowly can't aspire to. And they tell time by watches whose bands glitter of gold or platinum. Short of that, the bands are sleek smooth leather, but occasionally lizard. They do not wear Mickey Mouse watches.

Although not many men still wear hats for on-duty appearances (and certainly not indoors), when a powerful man travels outdoors he sometimes puts on a dark felt fedora—especially if he lacks a full head of hair—with the brim turned down to prove he knows all the amenities of the gentlemanly arts. A downturned brim portrays power; an upturned brim telegraphs whimsy or clownishness unsuitable to the projection of power.

SOUND BARRIERS

Back to Utopia for a brief sojourn.

When the wise abuse the law, they are more culpable than the ignorant who commit an unknowing transgression. This is just as true regarding the principles of dressing as it is in the field of jurisprudence.

For centuries, dress has divided rather than united people. Although it is not easy to do, try to delve beneath the surface of clothing, withholding judgment on those whom you would dismiss solely on the basis of their appearance. Judging people only by their dress is a step backward, not forward. Place your best self—which means the many facets of your self—before the world, of course, but don't foreshorten your horizons by keeping your sights too low. Communicative dress is but the first of many steps in the communication process. As powerful as clothing is, it exists to increase communication, not diminish it. Give clothing its due and then move on from there.

Maybe we didn't make a stopover in Utopia. Maybe it's possibly in the real world to make more of ourselves and still to have empathy for others. We'll never know if we don't try. Let's try.

LEFT. Long coats contribute to one's "bearing," often indicating "good breeding" (which is highly prized among the powerful and sometimes explains how they became powerful in the first place), since the "common man" will more often than not wear car coats or other styles that hover near or above his knees.

The chesterfield is certainly an uncommon coat style that has long been associated with classic formality. This particular one comes in a herringbone-tweed fabric, so it conveys less power than a dark, solid-colored coat.

A single-breasted blue blazer—with real gold buttons—is worn beneath the chesterfield, and this too lessens the power imagery: double-breasted blazers have more "weight."

On the other hand, the dark felt hat is very powerful indeed, and definitely tips the scales toward the powerful camp.

Sometimes a little power can go a long way. And sometimes it's advisable to sacrifice a bit of potent power imagery to prove one's humanity. Coat: Jeffrey Banks. Model: Todd Neuhaus.

POSTSCRIPT

When I was growing up in Northville, Michigan, I had no burning yen to be a men's-fashion writer. I doubt that few, if any, men of my age ever had such a boyhood ambition. And not many adult males today are itching to give it a try.

At social gatherings when I am introduced to someone new, the scenario is always the same, even if the dialogue varies a bit. In response to that ever-asked question "What do you do?" I see a glint of interest when I respond, "I'm a writer." But I know what's to follow. The next question is bound to involve what I write about, and when I say, "I write about the male appearance," invariably there's a momentary lull, and my new acquaintance looks both embarrassed and nervous, as if I might be carrying a rare but communicable virus. Should the person happen to know of my books, ease may be re-established, because the fact that they have sold well makes me legitimate again. But if the individual isn't familiar with my work, I note a continued uncertainty and can see the person asking him- or herself, What do you say to someone who writes about *the male appearance?* Life would be much easier if I were a sportswriter.

It's hard to write a book about men's fashion because some people believe there's no such thing. The time is still a long way off when society will cease to be suspicious of males who evidence great interest in their clothes.

I'm not suggesting that men *should* have "great interest" in how they dress. Like all else, clothing should be seen in perspective. But men should not be barred from experiencing the sense of pleasure that comes from looking their best because society is too near-sighted to recognize that that is a valid—if not a world-shakingly imperative—pursuit.

The reason that I write about the male appearance is this: I firmly believe that how we look affects how we feel about ourselves, and that in turn affects how others feel about us. We're not protoplasm; we are flesh and blood. As physical beings, we cannot ignore our physical trappings. To do so, I think, is wrong, because that leaves part of us undeveloped.

Fortunately, most young males aren't as rigid in their notions—prejudices might be the better word—about how they must, or should, dress as the men are who were born before the various libertarian movements made such great strides within the last few decades. It is to be hoped that our freer social climate will also free more and more males to escape stereotypes of behavior as well as dress, because the two are more intimately interrelated than many realize.

If this book helps a few men take a few more free steps, I'll be happy.

LEFT. Model: Troy Brown.

—C.H.

229

RESOURCES

No clothing should be purchased one day and discarded the next. The best outfits are composed of "lived-in" garb with a history of past associations with other garments, yet with enough versatility to form new associations as well. The old and the new should combine as good companions. With these thoughts in mind, the clothing selected to illustrate *Man Alive!* was culled from various sources. Some of the garments are old, some are new (or were so when the book was being compiled) and a great many of them are borrowed. A few pieces are one-of-a-kind or are items introduced more than a few seasons ago; these are not listed in the captions because they simply are not available today. On the other hand, many menswear manufacturers and designers lent their goods for this book, and those resources are credited in the captions. There is no guarantee that these particular garments are still available, but with perseverance, you will likely be able to locate similar styles. Of the resources listed below, those marked with an asterisk (*) are retail establishments. Designer names are listed when those names appear on clothing labels. The same holds true of the manufacturers listed. The assistance of all is greatly, greatly appreciated.

Garrick Anderson
   321 Fifth Avenue
   New York, N.Y.

Giorgio Armani
   650 Fifth Avenue
   New York, N.Y.

Artie & Cheech
   1466 Broadway
   New York, N.Y.

Jeffery Banks
   30 Rockefeller Plaza
   New York, N.Y.

Jhane Barnes
   21 West 38th Street
   New York, N.Y.

Basco
   15 West 55th Street
   New York, N.Y.

Basile
   41 Charlton Street
   New York, N.Y.

Hugo Boss
   714 Fifth Avenue
   New York, N.Y.

Canali Milano
   12 West 57th Street
   New York, N.Y.

Catalina
   1290 Avenue of the Americas
   New York, N.Y.

*D. Cenci
   801 Madison Avenue
   New York, N.Y.

Nino Cerruti
   26 West 56th Street
   New York, N.Y.

Cesarani
   12 East 53rd Street
   New York, N.Y.

*Charivari 72
   72nd Street & Columbus Avenue
   New York, N.Y.

*Charivari Men
   2339 Broadway
   New York, N.Y.

*Charivari Workshop
   81st Street & Columbus Avenue
   New York, N.Y.

Ron Chereskin
   22 West 19th Street
   New York, N.Y.

Cleo & Pat
   39 West 55th Street
   New York, N.Y.

Cole-Haan
   1370 Avenue of the Americas
   New York, N.Y.

Country Britches
   1290 Avenue of the Americas
   New York, N.Y.

Enrico Coveri
   745 Fifth Avenue
   New York, N.Y.

Cricketeer
   1290 Avenue of the Americas
   New York, N.Y.

Vicky Davis
   385 Fifth Avenue
   New York, N.Y.

*Descente
   655 Madison Avenue
   New York, N.Y.

Christian Dior
   261 Madison Avenue
   New York, N.Y.

Armand Diradourian
   8 Gramercy Park
   New York, N.Y.

Salvatore Ferragamo
   663 Fifth Avenue
   New York, N.Y.

Andrew Fezza
   37–39 West 28th Street
   New York, N.Y.

Float
   38 West 26th Street
   New York, N.Y.

Alan Flusser
   16 East 52nd Street
   New York, N.Y.

Roger Forsythe
   12 West 57th Street
   New York, N.Y.

Fratelli
   45 West 34th Street
   New York, N.Y.

Richard Gaines
   105 West 55th Street
   New York, N.Y.

Gleneagles
   1290 Avenue of the Americas
   New York, N.Y.

George Graham Gallery
   40 West 55th Street
   New York, N.Y.

Henry Grethel
   1271 Avenue of the Americas
   New York, N.Y.

Hart Schaffner & Marx
1290 Avenue of the Americas
New York, N.Y.

Hector Herrera
1466 Broadway
New York, N.Y.

Susan Horton
920 Broadway
New York, N.Y.

Alexander Julian
8 West 40th Street
New York, N.Y.

Robin Kahn
19 West 34th Street
New York, N.Y.

Laguna
245 Seventh Avenue
New York, N.Y.

Lee-Joffa Fabrics
979 Third Avenue
New York, N.Y.

G. Maislinger
145 West 55th Street
New York, N.Y.

*Matsuda
854 Madison Avenue
New York, N.Y.

*Missoni Boutique
836 Madison Avenue
New York, N.Y.

Palm Beach
1290 Avenue of the Americas
New York, N.Y.

*Parachute
121 Wooster Street
New York, N.Y.

Peter Barton's Closet
19 West 55th Street
New York, N.Y.

Piero Dimitri Couture
110 Greene Street
New York, N.Y.

Pinky & Diane
37 West 55th Street
New York, N.Y.

Pull Company
39 West 55th Street
New York, N.Y.

RGFM
105 West 55th Street
New York, N.Y.

Ray-Ban
c/o Hill & Knowlton
420 Lexington Avenue
New York, N.Y.

Austen Reed
1290 Avenue of the Americas
New York, N.Y.

Rooster Ties
17 East 37th Street
New York, N.Y.

Gianfranco Ruffini
1290 Avenue of the Americas
New York, N.Y.

Sahara Club
26 West 56th Street
New York, N.Y.

Samuelson & Abrams
261 Fifth Avenue
New York, N.Y.

*Screaming Mimi's
100 West 83rd Street
New York, N.Y.

Speedo
1411 Broadway
New York, N.Y.

Robert Stock
19 West 55th Street
New York, N.Y.

Michael Stromar
309 East 18th Street
New York, N.Y.

Bech Thomassen
220 East 60th Street
New York, N.Y.

*Trader
385 Canal Street
New York, N.Y.

U.S. Luggage
366 Fifth Avenue
New York, N.Y.

*Vittorio Ricci Boutique
645 Madison Avenue
New York, N.Y.

Egon von Furstenberg
800 Madison Avenue
New York, N.Y.

Lee Wright
c/o Oxford Industries
350 Fifth Avenue
New York, N.Y.

Ermenegildo Zegna
9 West 57th Street
New York, N.Y.